PREVAIL

DESTINY IMAGE BOOKS BY CINDY TRIMM

PUSH

The Soul Series:

The 40 Day Soul Fast

Reclaim Your Soul

The Prosperous Soul

PREVAIL

Discover Your Strength in Hard Places

CINDY TRIMM

DESTINY IMAGE® PUBLISHERS, INC.

P.O. Box 310, Shippensburg, PA 17257-0310

"Promoting Inspired Lives."

This book and all other Destiny Image and Destiny Image Fiction books are available at Christian bookstores and distributors worldwide.

Manuscript prepared by Rick Killian, Killian Creative, Boulder, Colorado. www.killiancreative.com

Cover design by Prodigy Pixel

For more information on foreign distributors, call 717-532-3040.

Reach us on the Internet: www.destinyimage.com.

ISBN 13 HC: 978-0-7684-0673-3

ISNB 13 TP: 978-0-7684-0907-9

ISBN 13 eBook: 978-0-7684-0674-0

For Worldwide Distribution, Printed in the U.S.A.

1 2 3 4 5 6 7 8 / 19 18 17 16 15

Prevail prē-vāl'
to be very powerful: to gain the victory:
to have greater influence or effect:
to overcome: to be in force: to succeed.

CONTENTS

A diamond…
It once was nothing special,
but with enough pressure and time,
becomes spectacular.
—SOLANGE NICOLE

FOREWORD

Have you ever imagined your life without problems, trials, or setbacks? I pose this thought-provoking question with the hope that you would give it some serious thought before answering "yes" or "no." I am sure that after much thought we would all be inclined to answer "yes" to this question. Who would decline to live a life that is "problem and stress free"? However, I am confident that if life did not challenge, stretch, and break us, we would never be who God intended us to be. Yes, we are fearfully and wonderfully made—and deep within we know that life's challenges come to help make us strong. As I reflect over my own life, I can honestly say that every setback, trial, and challenge that I have faced was only to refine me, mold me, and catapult me into my place of destiny.

In this life-changing book, *Prevail: Discover Your Strength in Hard Places*, you will be challenged to dig into God's Word, embrace adversity, and discover that every challenge you experience is part of God's masterful plan to position you for a life of victory. This book offers biblical revelation, real-life lessons, and practical strategies that will empower you to turn your trials into triumphs. As you read each page with a mindset of victory, you will discover God's divine plan for your life.

Dr. Cindy Trimm is recognized around the world as a renowned author, dynamic speaker, global strategist, and a trusted voice of hope. Her work is a testimony and indication that she is divinely attuned to the struggles and crises that many face. Brilliantly written, this book will engage you from start to finish. If you want to work on different aspects of your life or find strategies to live a better life, this book will give you a blueprint that will help you rebuild your life from the rubble of hurt, pain, and disappointment—while providing a spiritual compass designed to help you navigate through life's harsh terrains with personal integrity, courage, and resilience.

Prevail is a personal field guide you can use to reach the summit of your highest destiny, purpose, and promise. Dr. Trimm unveils the mystery of the diamond and uses its lessons as a powerful metaphor to shine light on your own hidden brilliance. The painstaking process that reveals a diamond's beauty and value offers life-transforming principles that will help anyone discover their strength in hard times. By remaining steadfast and standing strong in the midst of adversity, we all will eventually shine brighter than we ever imagined possible.

—BISHOP PAUL S. MORTON
Senior pastor, Changing a Generation FGBC, Atlanta, GA
Co-Pastor, Greater St. Stephen FGBC, New Orleans, LA
Presiding Bishop, Full Gospel Baptist Church Fellowship, Int'l

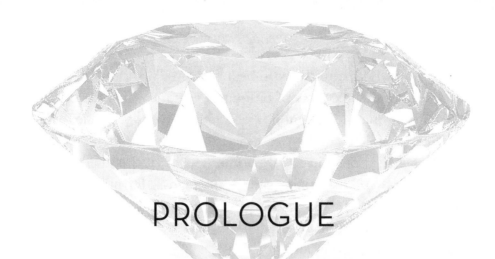

PROLOGUE

*A diamond is a chunk of coal that is
made good under pressure.*
—Henry Kissinger

You are a diamond in the rough. In fact, we all are.

While our contemporary culture assigns great worth to diamonds for their beauty and brilliance, a diamond is no more than a clump of carbon that refused to give in to pressure. Known for its beauty and held as a symbol of wealth and fortune, its importance has a long history. In the first century AD, the Roman naturalist Pliny stated, "Diamond is the most valuable, not only of precious stones, but of all things in this world."

Diamonds have been highly coveted since they were first discovered in southern India in the ninth century BC. Over a millennium later, when they found their way to markets in medieval Europe, they not only became fashionable among the European elite, but bejeweled the crowns of its nobility. To this day, diamonds have remained the most sought-after gem among people of affluence across the world. The ancients valued the stone for its exceptional strength, yet its brilliant luster is what continues to fascinate us most.

The diamond is indeed the hardest known natural material. Yet what makes the diamond strong is also what makes it so intriguingly beautiful. Intense heat and pressure cause carbon to crystalize over the course of billions of years. Formed deep within the earth's mantle, diamonds are brought close to the earth's surface by violent, molten eruptions—magma forcing its way up through deep volcanic fissures. The depths of this magma must originate where diamonds can be formed—100 miles or more below the earth's crust—at least three times the depth of source magma for most volcanoes.[1] This is a rare occurrence and why diamonds are so precious and costly.

As with any diamond, so it is with you. Life's upheavals bring your true worth and value hidden deep within to the surface—the heat inherent in your hardships, the pressure contained in your trials; it is from the confines of tight places the treasures within you emerge. If you don't allow your heart to become hard or your soul embittered, those hard places are where you will be transformed from the obscure and common into a distinctive, uncommon person of immense worth. Like a diamond exquisitely set, the world will witness your divine brilliance put on display by God Himself.

Imagine, three billion years ago, almost as old as the earth itself, a diamond began as a carbon deposit—dirty, brittle, combustible coal. Who would wear a piece of coal set in gold on their finger? Yet, through years of intense heat and extreme pressure, that sooty beginning gave way to beauty, brilliance, and value. Like you, its resilient nature makes it stable, pure, and strong. Endurance—the key feature that transforms rudimentary carbons into radiant carats—is a beautiful metaphor for the spiritual, mental, and emotional fortitude that is required for anyone to be transformed from ordinary to extraordinary.

This potential doesn't lie only in some of us, but in all of us. God uses the intensity of crisis and the force of adversity to rid us of the impurities that lead to mediocrity. It is the darkest places from which you emerge—like the dark before the dawn—that cause you to shine the brightest. The diamond has to be cut and polished to prepare it for acquisition. It is in the cutting that a diamond is made to shine so brilliantly. The more you are tested and tried, cut and polished, the more light you'll reflect. Not only that, but the more you overcome, the more valuable you ultimately become.

Your Problems Don't Define You

The word "diamond" originated from the Greek *adamas*, which translated means "unconquerable, unalterable, unbreakable, untamable." *Adamas* is a compound word formed from the prefix *a*, meaning "not," and *daman*, meaning "to conquer"; hence the concept of being unconquerable. Adam was the name given to the first created human being. Like a diamond, he was pulled from the earth. I believe he was called "Adam" because he represented the indomitable nature of mankind. When we speak of individuals as being adamant

> " *Hard places are where you will be transformed from the obscure and common into a distinctive, uncommon person of immense worth.* "

about something, we mean they are tough, resolute, immovable, unwavering, unswerving, uncompromising, determined, firm, and steadfast. How adamant you are about succeeding will determine the degree to which you shine—your *diamanté*, the degree to which you sparkle.

Because of the hardness of the stone, a diamond was once thought to be impossible to cut. However, over time technology gave way to the discovery that precision cutting made to a diamond with another diamond enhanced the diamond's brilliance. The more a diamond is cut, the brighter it sparkles; and like a diamond, the more life cuts away at us, the brighter we sparkle. As a diamond is masterfully chiseled to display the prismatic beauty of radiating light, so it is with you; when life cuts you the deepest and problems strike you the hardest, this is when the Master Jeweler is cutting and chiseling away at the superfluous so that you will reflect His light all the more brilliantly. The current pressure you are experiencing will bring the best out of you. You may begin this journey flawed, but you will end up fabulous!

Remember, God's strength is made perfect in your weakness.[2] Most people create the illusion of strength by leaning heavily on their defense mechanisms, masks, and façades—patterns of inauthenticity that erode their sense of worth. Many of us delude ourselves with the pretense of self-sufficiency, but the toll on our health, well-being, and relationships is a reminder that none of us are islands and of our need for total dependence on God. When we find our identity in Christ, have our being in Him, and lose our lives in His, that is when we reveal our diamond-like nature hidden deep within.

When you experience the fiery furnace of suffering and the overwhelming stress of problems—whether physical, financial, relational, or emotional—even as God is able to change a pebble into a pearl, a worm into a butterfly, an acorn into an oak tree, and a piece of coal into a diamond, and all of this in spite of the pressure, heat, and other opposing forces, He is able to bring the beauty and brilliance out of you as you overcome the temptation to give in to the pressure to remain as you are.

Transformation is not easy. Yet, no matter the difficulty, God is able to bring you through any furnace of affliction or fiery trial. Indeed, all things will work together for your good until your true worth shines as brilliant as a masterfully cut diamond. And like every diamond, you will prevail as you embrace the prospering power inherent in every problem, crisis, and adversity. Author Kevin Mullens writes:

> Those who suffer the greatest pressure, the most agonizing trials, the severest losses, the most mind-numbing isolation and the most debilitating infirmities, are being carefully formed in that unbearably lonely terrain by the One who Himself crafts His saints, His diamonds, the darlings of His care.[3]

Your problems don't define you; they refine you. I want you to embrace the power to prosper concealed within every problem.[4] It is from this vantage point that you will discover your innate strength in the most difficult of times. When you encounter a hard place, learn to tap in to the divine genius God deposited within you. In the worst of circumstances, allow your inner diamond-like essence, nature, and character to shine. You were divinely designed with the creative power to make sense out of chaos, to innovate your way out of setbacks, to produce your way out of scarcity, to revolutionize your way out from under oppression—you were designed to overcome,[5] for greater is He who is in you than any condition or circumstance.[6] Even in the harshest of situations, there is nothing too hard for God.[7]

DESTINED TO PREVAIL

Like a diamond, you are destined to prevail; even the roughest of diamonds are resilient. Diamonds, by their very nature, are impervious to being marred or scratched; they are used instead as instruments to cut into other hard materials. Likewise, don't allow a hard world to make its mark on you, but make your mark on it. Use every circumstance as an opportunity to prosper—to *prevail*.

> *Your problems don't define you; they refine you.*

What does it mean to prevail? I found it interesting that the word originated in the 1400s—about the same time diamonds found their way to Europe—and has its roots in the Old French *prevaleir*, derived from the Latin, *praevalere*, meaning "to be stronger, have greater power, be successful; be efficacious." The prefix *prae* means "before," and *valere* literally means "value or worth." If you think about it, there would be no "prevailing" if there weren't something first causing you to demonstrate your worth—some problem requiring a solution or deficit in need of your "value added proposition."

Therefore, before you are able to prevail, you must first be presented with a problem. Once the problem presents itself, you must be able to see a way through the problem. And once you see the way through, you must persevere until you have overcome the problem—or, as we commonly say, "proven what you're made of." Likewise, a diamond has no worth until it has been through the crucible of intense pressure and extreme heat—"been through the fire," so to speak. And it's not made to shine until it has been shaped, cut, and polished.

A DIAMOND'S WORTH

So what determines a diamond's worth? Its rare origins and how it is formed would seem to be enough. But there is more. There are actually four distinct characteristics that determine a diamond's value. These are known as the four "Cs"—clarity, color, carat, and cut.

A diamond's clarity is determined by the lack of impurities or "inclusions"—little specks or cloudy spots—while the color is actually evaluated by its *lack* of color, as in how clear or transparent it is. There are many colors of diamonds, but the most valuable ones are colorless. The word *carat* relates to its size or weight—a word originally derived from *carob*, because medieval merchants would use carob seeds as a countermeasure to determine a diamond's weight. Lastly, and perhaps most interesting of all, is how the diamond is cut. The number of cuts—or facets—determines the degree to which it sparkles.

The most famous and beautiful of all the ways a diamond can be cut is the "round brilliant-cut," more commonly known as "the Brilliant."

> A Brilliant is a diamond or other gemstone, cut in a particular form with numerous facets so as to have exceptional brilliance. The shape resembles that of a cone and provides maximized light return through the top of the diamond.[8]

Bear with me while I explain what makes a brilliant-cut diamond so brilliant. There are three main sections from top to bottom: The "crown," which is the top upper portion and is symmetrically round; the base, or "pavilion," which is the shape of a four-sided inverted pyramid; and the "girdle" which is a thin band around its circumference that divides the base from the crown (see diagram). Each component is comprised of a number of "facets"—or cuts.

> *So, like a diamond, you are a unique, multi-faceted being comprised of three main parts—spirit, soul, and body.*

The modern round brilliant has a total of fifty-seven facets; there are thirty-three on the crown and twenty-four on the pavilion.

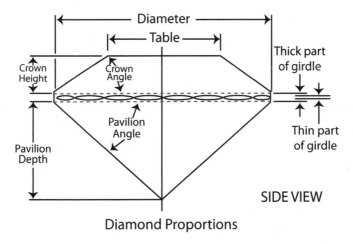

Diamond Proportions

Jesus walked on the earth thirty-three years, and at that age, died to crown us with His glory so we could shine with God's brilliance. Twenty-four is a priestly number; hence the apostle Peter's declaration that we are a royal priesthood. Additionally, even as there are a total of fifty-seven facets that comprise a brilliant diamond, there are also fifty-seven salient features of a human being, which mirror the play of light on the multifaceted surface of that diamond.

Only in recent decades have facets been added to the girdle, but these are not counted in the total number of cuts. While the facet count is standard, the proportions (crown height and angle, pavilion depth, etc.) are not universally agreed upon.[9]

Like a diamond, you are a unique, multi-faceted being comprised of three main parts—spirit, soul, and body. You could liken the crown of the diamond to your spirit, the "pavilion" to your physical being, and the "girdle" to your soul as it connects your spiritual and physical components. As we proceed, keep in mind that how the individual facets are cut into the pavilion—or four-sided base—determines how the light is reflected through the crown.[10]

Because I want you to understand how to prosper from your problems, how to capitalize on your circumstances, how to find deeper meaning and purpose in every difficulty, and how to endure for lasting success, I've divided this journey into four parts through which you will discover the prospering power of problems, perspective, purpose, and perseverance. And, because we're using the diamond as our primary metaphor, I am tying each of these to one of the characteristics that define a diamond's worth—clarity, color, carat, and cut.

Furthermore, because we've seen that a brilliant diamond is designed with a four-sided base cut with twenty-four facets, likewise we will assign six facets to each of our four sections. We will conclude with a crowning benediction offering thirty-three faith affirmations, or daily declarations, that you can proclaim over your life as you set your heart and mind to prevail. I encourage you to wear them as a crown over your thought life—a crown of honor and glory governing your words and deeds.

You are a masterpiece designed for greatness. You are a diamond destined to shine. Let's begin discovering your true brilliance as God cuts and chisels at your life through the circumstances you are going through.

The soul is placed in the body like a rough diamond,
and must be polished or the luster of it will never appear.
—DANIEL DEFOE

PART ONE:

CLARITY

THE PROSPERING POWER OF PROBLEMS

*There are unimaginable depths that
are released or develop
in those who have had to face and cope
with diversities and pressures.
Otherwise, one might remain shallow and superficial
and have no clue of what they are
really capable of becoming.*
—AUTHOR UNKNOWN

Facet One: CLARIFY

TAKE STOCK

When we long for life without difficulties,
remind us that oaks grow strong in contrary winds
and diamonds are made under pressure.
—PETER MARSHALL

Gaining clarity is one of the most powerful things you can do to get past roadblocks, overcome obstacles, heal your relationships, fix your finances, turn your business around, increase your productivity, get control of your health, or simply move ahead in life. Clarifying what is keeping you from moving forward, or where it is you want to go, will jump-start your momentum in any situation like nothing else can. Most of us have heard it said that "well begun is half done," and there is no better way to begin and end strong than to get clear on where you are now and what you need to do to get where you want to be.

Clarity springs forth from knowledge and understanding— both of which will require you to take an honest look at your circumstances and courageously take stock of the dynamics that have led to where you find yourself now. You cannot allow your current circumstances to blur your vision.

In this section, I want to help you get clarity on how you can grow and prevail through adversity in spite of any problem you currently face or might face in the future. You must learn to correctly read the signals a problem offers, how to interpret a recurring frustration, leverage the opposition you face, and capitalize on the lessons hidden in any given crisis. It is important to know when you need to change direction and when to stand your ground, what needs attention and what needs to be ignored. How can you know when to take hold of an issue and when you should let it go? What do you do when you don't know what to do?

COMPETING FOR ATTENTION

Today, when so many things are competing for your attention—the many problems in the world around you, the daily notifications from everyone you are connected to on Facebook or Twitter—how do you maintain your focus on what is most essential? More importantly, how can you build your capacity to expand your influence in order to effect change, grow, and accomplish your life goals? Gaining clarity is the first step in learning to prosper from any given problem.

Each challenge you face is a divine invitation for you to gain clarity concerning who you are and why you are here—your true identity and purpose.

When a diamond is examined for its clarity, a jeweler looks for impurities in the stone. These little flecks or murky areas are called "inclusions." The tiniest foreign particle will flaw the stone and greatly diminish its value. So what are the foreign particles in your life? What are those things cluttering your vision and encroaching on your purpose? Where are the murky areas hidden within you—the spots and blemishes—the inclusions you should exclude? These are the impediments and distractions that keep you living a lackluster existence. Take stock today. Don't allow the little foxes to spoil and cloud your brilliance. Take a thorough inventory of the habits, behaviors, and patterns that keep you stuck, the thoughts, words, and reactions that dampen your progress.[1]

What's interesting about a facet—the small cut made on the surface of a diamond—is how it reflects light. Each facet provides a unique reflection. They are not the source of light, but simply a reflection of it. The twenty-four facets we will shine light on throughout this book will each provide a unique reflection—a light that can reveal your own distinctive brilliance. Each challenge you face is a divine invitation for you to gain clarity concerning who you are and why you are here—your true identity and purpose.

Clarity is key to reflecting light. Getting clarity in a situation will allow you to adjust and make corrections, heal from old hurts, learn from mistakes and missteps, expand your problem-solving and crisis-management skills, and maximize your potential to inspire others. In the following chapters, we will explore some of the properties of problems that actually enable you to prosper.[2] This will provide a springboard and give some context to the prospering power of the other key principles presented in the next three sections of the book—perspective, purpose, and perseverance.

For now, take stock of where you are today. You can't start the process from where you are not—you can only start from where you are. Nobody can go backward in life to restart an old beginning, but you can start now to have a new ending. Without placing value on the choices you've made in the past, or regretting what you did to get where you are, simply embrace the fact that you have to start somewhere.

Begin by asking yourself some hard questions: What do I struggle with on a daily basis? What are the things that deflate and demotivate me, discourage or disappoint me, or disrupt or derail my best efforts? What pain do I want to eradicate? What situation do I want to mitigate? What lessons do I want to never repeat again? Are there recurrent shadows that creep up on me from my past or recurring cycles that I want to break, either personally, relationally, financially, socially, or professionally? Am I frustrated by my lack of progress or someone else's—or perhaps other people are holding me back? Or maybe you find yourself going from one bad relationship to the next. Are you prone to indecisiveness, making the wrong decisions, or failing to make any decision at all? Are you the type of person who starts something and never finishes? Do you tend to sabotage your own greatness and undermine your own success?

Take a few moments right now to consider what troubles you most. What are the "inclusions"—the dark or cloudy spots you're experiencing in your life—that need to become *exclusions*? Even a freckle can keep you from perfect clarity. Be completely transparent with yourself. Getting perfectly clear on where you are now will be critical in the next phase of discovering your brilliance.[3]

You are God's treasure formed before the foundations of the earth—you are His workmanship, brilliantly fashioned and formed.

So take out your journal and begin to deal with these questions head-on. Take stock and write down everything that comes to mind—everything you ultimately want to prevail over. Next, we will look at how each might be used to build your worth. Remember, *prevail* has its root in two Latin words: *prae*, meaning "before," and *valere*, "worth"—it is a cousin of the word *prosper* in its original meaning. The Latin *prospere* is translated "according to expectation" or "according to hope," and it literally means "for hope." So before you can prevail, you must actually prosper—for you will only discover your worth to the degree you expect or hope to, in accordance with your expectation that you are already worthy. If you read book number three in my Soul Series, *The Prosperous Soul*, you will learn that "to prosper" is what you do before any signs of prosperity show up in your life. It is much the same if you are to prevail. How will you avail—or make use of—your own brilliance *before* you experience the victory you seek?

TAKE STOCK OF YOUR LIFE

Let's begin by taking stock of your circumstances and your problems. What are you currently experiencing, and what are you hoping, or better yet expecting, to see as an alternative "best case scenario"? Identify what you perceive are the roadblocks or hindrances to achieving the results you hope—or expect—to produce. How do you need to *be* for those things to come to pass? Who do you need to become? How you see yourself—your own sense of identity—will determine your ultimate success. So while you're clarifying what circumstances or problems are keeping you from moving forward, take stock of your beliefs about the kind of person you are and what you are capable of achieving—be honest and clarify what you believe about yourself. Do you *believe* you are worthy? Do you *expect* to see yourself overcoming and prevailing? Have you embraced yourself as a valiant "prevailer"?

Get clear right now that not only are you worthy, but you are also of tremendous worth. You are God's treasure formed before the foundations of the earth—you are His workmanship, brilliantly fashioned and formed[4]—and for such a time you have emerged from the depths of eternity to surface in this present place, a rough diamond of tremendous value. Every problem, conflict, trial, hardship, and opposing force is shaping and polishing your brilliance, for without friction nothing comes clean or shines. So tell me, what is currently rubbing you the "wrong way" (or so you think)?

We are going to take a look at some typical "rubbing mechanisms" in the next several chapters. I will give you some clues for how to navigate seasons of struggle, address chronic relational issues, learn from your failures, and broaden your capacity to inspire change not only in yourself but in others who will see you as their example and gain hope for their own lives.

Every problem is a gift—
without problems we would not grow.
—Anthony Robbins

READ THE SIGNS

Problems are not stop signs, they are guideposts.
—ROBERT H. SCHULLER

Without problems, you would never change. And though it doesn't seem to make sense, without setbacks things would always stay the same. Setbacks, shake-ups, and breakups are wake-ups. They may be challenging, but it takes a challenge to cause us to grow. Overcoming resistance is how you become stronger.

Anyone who has ever been to the gym will tell you that resistance training is the only way to strengthen your muscles—and that without some degree of resistance in your day-to-day moving about and doing things, your muscles, your mind, and ultimately your life would atrophy. If you're not continually rising to a new challenge, reaching for new heights, you're stagnating. In order to grow you must stretch yourself— your mind, body, will.

The key is not to get stuck overanalyzing your situation or overwhelmed by the resistance you feel or seduced into believing you are trapped by your circumstances—because you are not. There are cycles that can keep you running in circles—toxic relationships, counterproductive environments, addictive habits you'll need to take authority over, and dry wilderness seasons you'll want to find your way out of. God does not allow these into your life for your destruction, but to get you out of where you are now to bring you to someplace better. He allows discomfort so you can settle once and for all that you deserve better. Notice I said, "God allows." Many of these situations we find ourselves in are of our own doing, not God's. That means if you have the power to create a particular situation, then you have the power to eliminate that situation.

To prosper from your problems, you have to be convinced that not only do you deserve better but you also have the power to do and be better—you have the power to create the change you want to see. Learning to view your difficult situations as signposts is vital to your growth. They are tools you can use to redirect, change course, or plot a new destination. Problems are simply indicators giving feedback, like a wind gauge or a compass. As the old saying goes, "Don't shoot the messenger."

> *Setbacks, shake-ups, and breakups are wakeups.*

PROBLEMS PRESENT OPPORTUNITIES TO REVIEW YOUR LIFE STRATEGY

Problems have a way of jolting us out of our usual routines into defining moments. The experience we receive from facing our problems rather than running from them is of invaluable benefit. No matter how bad things seem, if you approach problems as learning opportunities you will see your way through them. Ask yourself, "What am I to learn?" and, "How can I use this to assist me in defining the new path I will take to fulfill my purpose and maximize my potential?"

You have to ask yourself the hard questions and force yourself to answer without justifying, rationalizing, or explaining circumstances away. Don't get too caught up with, "How did I get here?" as much as asking yourself:

- Where do I really want to be?

- What road must I take to get there?

- What are my options?

- What is the best decision I can make based on these options?

You will be tempted to overanalyze, second-guess, and go around and around like a plane circling, never able to land. Don't get trapped by the paralysis of analysis. Never seek justification. Refuse to use people as alibis. This is your life. You must own the decision for the change you seek and then harness the power of your will to make it happen. If you don't like your life, change it. Getting advice from people you trust and finding an objective opinion or two before you decide to act is fine—but then you must act decisively and with conviction. In the worst instance, you will encounter a roadblock, another problem, and yet another opportunity to reflect, reevaluate, and redirect—another opportunity to improve and grow.

> *To prosper from your problems, you have to be convinced that not only do you deserve better, but you also have the power to do and be better.*

There is tremendous power available to those who are willing to stop, take stock, and simply reflect in the midst of life's circumstances. I have discovered that just taking *me moments* to think and record my thoughts helped me through the most turbulent times.

Napoleon Hill's book *Think and Grow Rich* starts with the word *think*. He postulates that everything in life starts and finishes with our thoughts. The quality of our thoughts determines the quality of our lives. Thinking is something you don't need a master's degree to do; it's absolutely free. So why not think for a change? Your life can only go where your mind is willing to take it—it's a matter of your will. So, knowing that you are fully able, are you fully willing? Use your present difficulties as an opportunity to review your life strategy. What got you here will never be enough to take you someplace different.

Problems Are Cycle Breakers

Quite simply, as Dr. Henry Cloud explains, "We change our behavior when the pain of staying the same becomes greater than the pain of changing. Consequences give us the pain that motivates us to change." In other words, consequences make us *willing* to change. And the power of will is especially needed when we find ourselves trapped in a negative cycle of self-defeating habits, thought patterns, or reactions.

Cycles have to be broken if you are to free yourself from the centrifugal force of the whirlpools they create. If you are to get out of the present lifestyle you are living, you have to change the cycles and patterns that have created that life. Randy Pausch, with only six months left to live, authored a book entitled *The Last Lecture*. In it, he wrote:

> The brick walls are there for a reason. The brick walls are not there to keep us out. The brick walls are there to give us a chance to show how badly we want something. Because the brick walls are there to stop the people who don't want it badly enough.[1]

Problems are like those brick walls. If you accept your habits as unalterable and unchangeable, you will never break through into a new way of living. However, if you embrace problems for their intrinsic value and power to transform you from within rather than their extrinsic impact on your circumstances, they can be the catalysts that rupture old cycles and propel you forward.

You have the prerogative to call a "time out" and to decide when enough is enough. Because you'll always get what you are willing to put up with, problems often come to push you beyond what you will allow so you will make a change. When faced with problems that seem insurmountable, however, you must resist the desire to "check out," instead going for the gold, digging deep, and playing "full out." For this is when winning points are scored and touchdowns are made.

Cycles of failure *can* be replaced with cycles of success. Old cycles of abuse, oppression, and misuse *can* be replaced with new cycles of respect, accomplishment, and honor. Old cycles of rejection *can* be replaced with new cycles of recognition and celebration. Poverty *can* be replaced with prosperity. Cycles of addiction, deviance, and perversion *can* be replaced with cycles of discipline, decency, and wholesomeness. Even criminal behavior can be replaced with honesty, moral conduct, and an honorable lifestyle.

> *Confronting and solving the problems before you can be the impetus to reverse the downward cycle you are currently experiencing into an upward cycle of abundance, growth, success, and prosperity.*

Living hand-to-mouth *can* be replaced with living from an abundance of reserves, having more than enough, and building for the future.

Confronting and solving the problems before you can be the impetus to reverse the downward cycle you are currently experiencing into an upward cycle of abundance, growth, success, and prosperity. For, as stated the poet Tuli Kupferberg, "When old patterns are broken, new worlds emerge."

PROBLEMS MARK THE ENDING OF ONE SEASON AND THE BEGINNING OF ANOTHER

There is always a transitional process that occurs to take you from one state into another. When people change, it is usually because their negative emotional patterns have become too painful for them to tolerate or because their entire world seems to be falling apart. This period is usually characterized by disintegration, disillusionment, and disorientation, which are typically experienced in the stepping out from the old and into the new.

Many psychotherapists refer to this as the "limbo of chaos and uncertainty," a state from which you are motivated to change by the persuasive nature of the very pain you are enduring. It comes at the point you decide that you have had enough of struggling, depression, constant anxiety, and inner turmoil—when you decide that enough is enough. This happens when you become aware and appreciative of the fact that you are on a dead-end course leading nowhere; the end of which may lead to emotional, spiritual, and even physical death. It is at that point in your life when you are finally sick and tired enough of being sick and tired that you change. You have hit your personal rock bottom and are willing to risk the pain of change, knowing there's nowhere to go but up. Only when you are willing to take that risk of thinking and acting in new ways will you begin to see new life emerge.

Regrettably, there are those who have to fall apart quite badly before they are willing to put the pieces of their lives back together in a new and different pattern. Fortunately, you will not be mentioned among them because you're here now reading this book. Instead, you will be among those who read the signs and correct your course, growing stronger and wiser for the effort. This time of transition can be unsettling at best, but you have the mental and spiritual strength to push beyond pain, discomfort, fear of the unknown, and the seduction of giving up all together. Resilience is what I call it.

Laura Hillenbrand, author of the best sellers *Seabiscuit* and *Unbroken,* had this to say about resilience and the transitional experience that ushered her from one season into the next:

> It started in a very typical way—very suddenly. Prior to that, I was a straight A student, perfectly healthy. I was a very serious athlete. One evening I was driving back from

spring break. I think I ate something that was bad earlier that day and I developed food poisoning.

For about two weeks, I was very sick. With CFS [Chronic Fatigue Syndrome], it's typical to have a triggering problem. It could be food poisoning, a bad flu, or pneumonia. I woke up two weeks after getting the food poisoning and I simply couldn't sit up in bed.

The biggest problem has been exhaustion. I've spent about six of the last fourteen years completely bedridden. At times, I have been unable to bathe myself. I have gotten so bad I couldn't really feed myself and a couple of times I needed someone to spoon feed me. I have had trouble rolling over in bed....

I spent the first year of my illness pretty much bed-bound and when I began to improve a little bit in 1988, I needed some way to justify my life. I had an idea watching the Kentucky Derby—[it was] something I could write about that hadn't been discussed much. So I wrote an essay and mailed it to *Turf & Sport Digest*.[2]

And that was the start of what became *Seabiscuit* and sealed her destiny as a writer. Despite the continued hardships of her disease, her books have inspired millions.

Life can sometimes feel like being in a boat making its way through a storm—you must adjust the sails based on the winds. Some winds are gale force winds that threaten your health, relationships, finances, and sensibility. In the midst of your storm you must choose the life you want and then adjust your actions—and *reactions*—to ensure that your life continues to flow in the direction of purpose and toward the haven of self-actualization no matter what. You do not have to be a victim of circumstances nor controlled and conditioned by the adverse winds emanating from the prevailing culture, your environment, or even your own personal setbacks. You do not have to live as a demographic catastrophe, a statistical disaster, nor among the clutter of the common who claim, "The odds are ever stacked against me, so I cannot succeed, prosper, or overcome."

Defy the odds. Distinguish yourself as an overcomer. You have weathered many storms, proving that you are indeed "sea-worthy" and "storm-resistant." Promise me that when you want to give in or give up, you will keep telling yourself, "I am stronger than this. I can weather any storm that confronts me. I did it before and I can do it once more." It was Thomas Edison who once said, "Our greatest weakness lies in giving up. The most certain way to succeed is always to try just one more time."

PROBLEMS BEG THE QUESTION, "WHAT DO YOU REALLY WANT?"

The Bible tells the story of an impotent man who was trapped by cultural conditioning and self-defeating beliefs for thirty-eight years.[3] He thought he had to wait for an angel to stir the water in the pool and then to be the first one in, even though he had no physical way of getting into the pool. The truth was, however, that he didn't need to get into the pool; he needed to meet Jesus.

You can change your future by viewing your current condition as a transition into a new season.

When he met Jesus, everything changed. Jesus asked him, "What do you want?" The man was prompted by God to decide for himself what it was he really wanted. Do you want to become a victim of your circumstances, or do you want a better life? Jesus basically said, "So be it according to your desire." With that divine directive, the man was empowered to get up and walk into the future of his choosing and to live the life of his dreams—and so can you.

Could things be the way they are because you are the way you are? What one thing can you change that can change everything?

Like the impotent man who gained his mobility, it is a matter of mind over matter.

Right where you are, although you cannot change the past and you might not have the power to alter your present, you can change your future by viewing your current condition as a transition into a new season. Something has to come to an end in order for something new to begin. You cannot hold on tightly to the old and grasp the new at the same time. You must release the old in order to embrace the new. You might have to do things differently, but do not give in to the thought that your life has to remain the same, and that nothing will ever change. Get up. Take up that thing that represents your dream and put feet to it. Remember your feet will never take you where your mind is unwilling to go.

Are there some signs in your life signaling you to make a change? What is the nature of your particular signposts and how can you read them to make a course correction? Are there any cycles or patterns you need to break? Are you sensing a change of season? Is there a decision you need to make? Use this opportunity to get clear on at least one thing you need to take action on today.

> *The beauty is that through disappointment*
> *you can gain clarity, and with clarity comes*
> *conviction and true originality.*[4]
> —CONAN O'BRIEN

Facet Three: HEAL

ADDRESS CHRONIC ISSUES

Pressure can burst a pipe,
or pressure can make a diamond.
—ROBERT HORRY

Understanding how to read and respond to some of the major signposts we all experience in the course of life is only the beginning in your quest for clarity. Some of the problems that can cause you the most grief and create some really difficult situations are those related to people. I realize that's no surprise to many of us, but at the same time most of us underestimate the role that various people and relationships play in our lives.

Unhealthy roles, toxic relationships, and sabotaging communication patterns can be insidiously destructive. Subtle dysfunctions can lead to chronic emotional pain. I go into great detail about how to take back your personal power and heal your relationships in the second book of my Soul Series, entitled *Reclaim Your Soul.* I will only touch briefly here on how to recognize the relationship issues that keep you from thriving—and how those problems can work toward your advantage if dealt with correctly.

Because we are all growing and changing every moment of every day, so will our relationships. At the same time, we are designed to be in constant relationship with other people. In fact, our emotional health depends and even hinges upon it. When our relationships are unhealthy, so is our emotional health—the two go hand in hand. Our emotional state is so tied to those we are connected with that we will take upon ourselves the problems and issues of those we are closest to. We are most certainly called upon to empathize and share in the burdens of others—that is a very good thing—but those relationships can become unhealthy if we don't steward them correctly.

You must guard your emotional well-being not only to maintain our own ability to prosper but also if you are to be that pillar, wise confidant, or source of comfort in the hour of a friend's need. You want to maintain your "peace of mind" so you are always emotionally available to provide support for your loved ones. That will require you to negotiate within those same relationships to have your own needs met. Learn to quickly address those areas that sap your energy not only in the context of your relationships but in your home environment, workplace, and community Think about it. If you were able to articulate your personal needs and have them met, who would you be—who might that enable you to become if you could stop the emotional leaks?

> *Learn to quickly address those areas that sap your energy not only in the context of your relationships but in your home environment, workplace, and community.*

PROBLEMS CAN SIGNAL THE NEED TO RENEGOTIATE YOUR RELATIONSHIPS

The source of most of our emotional leaks will be the interactions we have with those closest to us. Sometimes you will outgrow a certain relationship because that person is not ready for *you* to grow. When you are looking to make some adjustments, to shift some things in your life—to develop and change so you can get to the next level—certain relationships will become toxic to you. Yet, even though a relationship is stripping you of your self-confidence, energy, or valuable time, those relationships can still be very difficult to sever. Although they may be causing you a great deal of pain, there are psychological ties that keep you bound to those relationships. More often than not, those ties must be undone if you are to move on.

The famous motivational speaker, Jim Rohn, gives the following counsel:

> You must constantly ask yourself these questions: Who am I around? What are they doing to me? What have they got me reading? What have they got me saying? Where do they have me going? What do they have me thinking? And most important, what do they have me becoming?[1]

Then ask yourself the big question: Is that okay? Your life does not get better by chance; it gets better by change.

I would add that your life gets better by choice—you must *choose* to change. You must choose to surround yourself with people who can help you get to the next level—who have the capacity to nurture your greatness. By the same token, says General Colin Powell, "The less you associate with some people, the more your life will improve." The more you tolerate compromise in others, the more you will tolerate compromise in yourself. Taking the road of least resistance may seem a good option for some, but is it the road that will take you where you want to be? An important attribute of successful people is their intolerance of complacency and small thinking. Raise the bar on what you expect from yourself and others.

As you grow, your associations will naturally change. Some of your friends will unconsciously want to hold you back from success because they don't want to make the changes you are trying to make. Misery loves company. Many alcoholics or those with similar addictions will have codependent relationships wherein they may talk about wanting to change, but allow others to enable their self-destructive behavior. General Powell famously observed, "Friends that don't help you climb will want you to crawl. Your friends will either stretch your vision or choke your dream. Those that don't increase you will eventually decrease you."

Ponder this: Why would you receive counsel from someone who isn't successful in the area they are offering advice? Avoid discussing your problems with someone incapable of contributing to the solution; those unable to succeed themselves always seem first in line to tell you how you should or should not do things, or why changing won't make a difference. If they knew better than you, they would be doing better than you. Be careful whom you allow to speak into your life; you are certain to get the wrong direction when you share your dreams with people who don't have any of their own. Don't follow someone who isn't going anywhere or who has never been where you are trying to go. There is an old Chinese proverb: "To know the road ahead, ask those coming back."

Be cautious where you stop to inquire for directions along the road of life. In the wise words of General Powell: "Never receive counsel from unproductive people." Never discuss your challenges with people who are overwhelmed with their own. Wise is the person who fortifies his or her life with the wisdom from those who bear the proof. Who around you has a testimony of overcoming? Who around you has a passion for more and the fruit in their lives to prove it? Remember, you will resemble those with whom you assemble.

Don't follow someone who isn't going anywhere or who has never been where you are trying to go.

There is another well known saying that applies here: "If you run with wolves, you will learn how to howl. But if you associate with eagles, you will learn how to soar to great heights. A mirror reflects a man's face, but what he is really like is shown by the kind of friends he chooses."

A simple but true fact of life is that you become like those with whom you closely associate—the good and the bad. This applies to family as well as friends. Of course, you can't trade family members in for better ones, but you can choose whose counsel to take to heart and whose to simply "take under advisement." Appreciate and be thankful for your family, for they will always be your family no matter what, but some of them will likely need your help and wisdom more than you'll need theirs.

PROBLEMS MAY SIGNAL THE NEED FOR NEW ASSOCIATIONS

There is another bit of wisdom that goes something like this: "People that hold our ten-foot ladder often don't have the capacity to hold our twenty-foot ladder."[2] Problems might not only be a red flag of the "toxic mindsets" you're acquiring from unbeneficial relationships, but they may also point to your need to develop new relationships with people who can help you solve the very problems you are perplexed by.

Find the people who have the capacity for where you are going, not where you came from. Find your tribe and thrive. Find the ones who pitch to your strength rather than magnify your weaknesses or flaws. Here is a list of the types of relationships you should cultivate no matter where you are now:

- Friends who have similar interests, values, and goals.

- Thought leaders in your industry (those who have been where you are trying to go).

- Coaches[3] who will challenge you to hone specific skills, construct a dynamic vision for your life, and create a plan for maximizing your potential.

- Mentors[4] who can give you guidance and constructive feedback.

- Networks and associations that will help you grow and develop professionally.

- Legal and financial advisers who can help you build and protect your assets.

- Industry experts who can help you develop your "brand" so you can improve your marketability and increase your profits (lawyers, bankers, P.R., marketing experts, accountants, etc.).

- Brand evangelists who promote you and your products/goods/services.

- Brand protectors who do not allow you to compromise your greatness, credibility, unique value-added proposition or authenticity.

- A circle of trust with whom you can pour your heart out, share your dreams and vision; those upon whom you can lean on for personal advice, and who act as a sounding board.

Seek out and cultivate enriching relationships—they are the best investment you can make in your future. Except for one primary relationship that you should pursue above all others: Your relationship with God.

PROBLEMS DRAW YOU CLOSER TO GOD

The problems we experience in life are allowed by God in order to draw us closer to Him. I really can't say it any better than the apostle Paul:

Distress that drives us to God does that. It turns us around. It gets us back in the way of salvation. We never regret that kind of pain. But those who let distress drive them away from God are full of regrets, end up on a deathbed of regrets.

And now, isn't it wonderful all the ways in which this distress has goaded you closer to God? You're more alive, more concerned, more sensitive, more reverent, more human, more passionate, more responsible. Looked at from any angle, you've come out of this with purity of heart.[5]

Distress that drives you to God turns you around. When you are driven closer to God, you're more alive. That's prospering power in action. Of all the ways problems help you to prosper, it's in how they can bring you closer to your heavenly Father, drawing you nearer to Him in intimacy. Have you brought your problems before the Lord? What are some of the issues you've been holding back and harboring in the depths of your heart? Is it time to dig them up and give them over to God?

> *Seek out and cultivate enriching relationships—they are the best investment you can make in your future.*

Think about your relationships for a moment, and then pray over those that need healing. Ask God to show you which ones you should move away from, and then pray for the wisdom and grace to step back peaceably and lovingly. Inquire of the Lord for insight regarding new relationships you should pursue, or healing old relationships you may have discarded—and then pray for divine opportunities and favor to engage those individuals. Pay attention as the Spirit of God is always working to position you to be in the right place at the right time to meet the right people. Your part is to be discerning and add value.

How you address and cultivate healthy relationships can be a source of great healing, peace, and prosperity. Learn to evaluate, identify, and "renegotiate" the terms of your associations on an ongoing basis—speaking the truth in love[6]—and always, always leaning on the God of love for His direction and guidance.

PREVAIL

Peace is not the absence of affliction,
but the presence of God.
When we put our cares in His hands,
He puts His peace in our hearts.
—AUTHOR UNKNOWN

Facet Four: LEARN

DISCOVER YOUR STRENGTHS

Strength does not come from winning.
Your struggles develop your strengths.
When you go through hardships
and decide not to surrender,
that is strength.
—ARNOLD SCHWARZENEGGER

Every problem is a learning opportunity. It's in the midst of life's crucibles that we learn who we are and what we're capable of, and ultimately where we need to grow. Every struggle builds strength, if for no other reason than because our weaknesses are exposed. But as long as we don't surrender, we will become stronger than we were before entering the struggle. The key is to keep learning and adjusting, and to learn and adjust again…and again and again. With every reiteration you become better.

The same is true for a business, research lab, or sports team. There will be trial followed by error, and yet another error and another trial. Those who are able to evaluate and adjust best are the trendsetters, market leaders, Nobel laureates, trophy winners, and history-makers.

Problems Challenge You to Get Stronger

Yes, you will fail. Strangely enough, experience has taught me that I failed the most when I aimed the lowest. When I dared to raise the bar on my own performance, my rate of success increased. Yes, you will discover shortcomings. I discover more as I grow older. And yes, you may even trip and fall at times. But with every hill and hiccup comes an opportunity to improve your life. When you encounter a weakness, address it head-on and turn it around to build your mental, emotional, intellectual, spiritual, and even physical fortitude to be ready for the next challenge. Anticipate and prepare for opposition.

Boldly facing obstacles and learning to continually navigate around them—or bulldoze through them—will strengthen and enable you to overcome any weakness you may be facing. What used to knock you flat before, you will begin to handle with greater ease.

Your own physiology shows you that strength cannot be developed without opposition. Persevering through difficulty is the only thing that will make you stronger. Persistent perseverance will keep your life—your potential, your purpose, and your dreams—from atrophying.

Problems Develop Character

Helen Keller beautifully summed up the power of a problem to prosper you when she stated, "Character cannot be developed in ease and quiet. Only through experiences of trial and suffering can the soul be strengthened, vision cleared, ambition inspired, and success achieved."

Problems force us to evaluate where we are and how we have been living. This process helps us to better focus on identifying our core values and to move forward with greater integrity. Character building starts in the cradle and ends in the grave—and it peaks in times of duress and trial. Oscar Wilde once said, "Every little action of the common day makes or unmakes character, and that therefore what one has done in the secret chamber, one has some day to cry aloud from the housetop."[1]

It is those character-building moments that make you the person you are. The key to successful living is to keep growing and to challenge yourself to dig deep within your mental, emotional, and spiritual reservoir to find the hidden stream of courage to face the challenge before you. You will not really know the stuff you are made of until opposition comes and you hoist the sails of your values and principles and navigate through opposing forces. Only then will you travel the seemingly unnavigable waters that lead to a haven of happiness, peace, success, and prosperity.

> *Problems force us to evaluate where we are and how we have been living.*

PROBLEMS CLARIFY YOUR NONNEGOTIABLES

Problems are always a values clarification experience. By that I mean they help you decide what you can let go of or lose and what you cannot. The ones you give away or give up are negotiable—those you must absolutely keep are your nonnegotiables. Here is a brief list of some of the values I have found to be nonnegotiable in my life:

- My personal relationship with God

- Family life

- Prayer and meditation

- Peace

- Respect

- Joy

- Harmonious and healthy living

49

- Kindness

- Peace

- Honesty

- Individuality

- Freedom

- A good reputation

- Influence

- Purpose

- Moral clarity

- Ethical conduct in personal, work, and business affairs

Knowing what you value is like having an internal compass guiding you through life. It is your personal GPS giving you direction and continuous course correction. Knowing what you can let go of and what you can't will also allow you to lighten the ship in rough seas and know you will be none the worse when you finally hit shore. Things and money can always be replaced—character and close relationships cannot.

Things and money can always be replaced—character and close relationships cannot.

Stop and think for a moment about what you would consider your nonnegotiables. What can you learn about your desires, values, and purpose from them? What do they tell you about the direction your lifestyle, routines, and relationships are taking you? How do they strengthen you? Now prioritize them. Which are most essential? Which are not serving your greater purpose or dreams?

PROBLEMS PRESENT YOU WITH EMPOWERING CHOICES

Your power to choose is made most evident when you face a problem or impasse. Such times may challenge and shake you to the core, but you must resist the tendency to think a particular challenge has come to break you down. Instead, "fear not and only believe,"[2] for it has been divinely presented to help you break*through* into new realms of authority, influence, prosperity, and joy—to reveal who you really are and what you're truly capable of.

We all do what we do in the midst of our challenges, trials, and temptations because we are creatures of habit. You will always do the things you have always done until you realize you have other options. There is always an alternative response—this is why praying for insight and revelation (a "revealing") is so important.

You may be tempted to believe that your current state of relational or financial affairs, your emotional or physical condition, or even a national or economic crisis will finally be the end of you. Maybe you feel that whatever you are facing has already done you in. However, if you will look at things differently, you will see that rather than destroying you, the issues you face merely reveal your truest, most fundamental self. They peel away the distractions; they eliminate the facades—all that remains is the strength of your character and the divine spark hidden within that will elevate you to a better way of living.[3]

> *You will see that rather than destroying you, the issues you face merely reveal your truest, most fundamental self.*

Challenges realign you to what is truly important in life. They expand the horizon of your vision for what is possible. If you lose your resolve, you will never see it, but if you choose to stand resolute, you will see that what you thought would defeat you is a new opportunity to press forward and grow more like who God has called you to be.

Life can be like a baseball game. It has a way of throwing hard-balls and curveballs—sliders, sinkers, cutters, knuckleballs, and the like—trying to strike us out. Sometimes you swing and miss. Sometimes you hit a fly ball that an outfielder catches. Other times the pitcher hits you with the ball and you get a free pass to first. When you strike out—not *if* but *when*—you have to make the choice to quit or stay in the game. The next time you're up to bat, you may just hit a homerun...yet even then, the best players still fail six or seven times out of ten. You could begin to lack confidence, or you could boldly step up to the plate trusting your next hit will make all the difference.

Refuse to give up because you feel awkward, uncomfortable, or even if it hurts. We all hurt at times. Decide today that from now on, no matter how painful or devastating the impact of the blow, you will always get back in the ring or step up to the plate and swing again. Refuse to hide in the dugout, or worse, retreat to the bleachers and sit among the masses as just another specta-tor. Get back in the game. Play full out. Refuse to withdraw to the sidelines.

You are the headliner in your life story. Go for the gold. Win the Oscar. Take the prize. As Paul put it:

> *Do you not know that those who run in a race all run, but one receives the prize? Run in such a way that you may obtain it. ...Therefore I run thus: not with uncertainty. Thus I fight: not as one who beats the air. But I discipline my body and bring it into subjection, lest, when I have preached to others, I myself should become disqualified.*[4]

If Shakespeare's metaphorical description of life is true, and if indeed "all the world's a stage," dare to be the leading actor—push to be the protagonist in the unfolding drama of your life story. If you don't like where you are at the moment, rewrite your script. Cast yourself as a different character. Change your tragedy into a comedy, your drama into a celebration of success. Refuse to play a supporting role—step into the limelight and make something special happen! You have the power to choose.

> *First, say to yourself what you would be;*
> *and then do what you have to do.*[5]
> —EPICTETUS

BUILD YOUR CAPACITY

*You are at this moment standing in the middle
of your own "acres of diamonds."*[1]
—EARL NIGHTINGALE

I hope you are beginning to see that seldom is there progress without facing and clarifying problems. The seed of greatness within you will only break open and germinate when heated by the fire of challenges. No wonder James advises us to *"count it all joy"*[2] when we face hardships, and why the writer of Hebrews encourages us to look to Jesus, *"who for the joy that was set before Him endured the cross."*[3] Of all the hard places ever experienced, it was in Jesus's sacrifice on the cross—but wouldn't you agree the resurrection power that resulted expanded His capacity to change the world?

If you want to build your capacity to do anything, you'll have to harness the power of a problem to expand you.

PROBLEMS ARE CAPACITY BUILDING EXPERIENCES

I wonder if Jabez was surprised when, after he cried out to God, *"Enlarge my territory,"*[4] the first thing that came along the next day was a problem.

Problems and hardships increase your capacity emotionally, spiritually, professionally, economically, socially, and personally. If you allow them to, problems will broaden your sphere of influence, context, and scope—they will enlarge your territory. They will deliver you from limiting beliefs about what you are capable of.

Gaining the conviction and power to become and accomplish everything that you are wired to be and do takes courage—it forces you to see yourself from Heaven's perspective and not through the eyes of people. It opens your heart to what is possible.

> *If you allow them to, problems will broaden your sphere of influence, context, and scope—they will enlarge your territory.*

Dutch painter Vincent Van Gogh said it this way, "As we advance in life it becomes more and more difficult, but in fighting the difficulties the innermost strength of the heart is developed."[5] Open your heart and give yourself permission to grow more, to love more, and to give more—and allow others permission to do the same. The more those around you grow, the more you will too.

PROBLEMS DEMAND NEW SKILL SETS

New seasons require new strategies, and new strategies require new skills. My personal trainer once said, "Do the same, get the same; do different, get different." I have good and bad news for you. Here's the bad new first: When you attempt to develop or acquire new skills, you will feel the force of opposing winds. Here's the good news: Even when the wind is blowing against you, it is possible to position the boat of your life—your lifeboat—so that you can move against it. By adjusting the sail, you can create a unique dynamic where the easiest direction for the boat to move is into the wind. The technique is called "tacking," and it can be likened to squeezing a wet bar of soap with two hands, causing it to shoot out in a direction perpendicular to both opposing forces.

In tacking you use the strength of the opposing forces to propel you in the direction you want to go.

You are a magnificent vessel filled with precious cargo—gifts, talents, and skills—that the world needs. Hidden within you are brilliant ideas, creative solutions, and insightful strategies for solving economic problems, social ills, world dilemmas, and the like. The winds may be against you, but you can't give up. People need you. You must learn how to navigate the storms of life to get where you need to be. No successful person I have ever met has gotten there without some contrary winds along the way. Life is rarely smooth sailing, especially if you want to remain on the cutting edge and make a difference in the world. By definition, helping others means sailing into turbulent waters. If you are to effect change, you must know how to sail through your personal storms and help others to do the same.

Tacking isn't accomplished by the angle of the sail alone. Sailboats overcome opposing winds by having another physical object below the water line. This may take the form of a keel, rudder, or centerboard. Thus, the physical portion of the boat below the water line functions as a "second sail." Your proverbial rudder is your belief system—your core beliefs—that may not be visible on the surface, but nonetheless affect your progress and direction in life.

Life is filled with contrary forces. Any person who has ever attempted anything can testify to that. If you are going to accomplish anything of significance, there are going to be times you will have to "sail against the wind" as you develop new skills. Such winds can blow externally or internally—driven by forces without as well as by forces within. There are the naysayers, cultural constraints, the status quo, friends, family, competitors, and the prevailing atmosphere or environment in which you live. Within, there are your own doubts, fears, insecurities, and emotions that can catch you by surprise and veer you off course. These forces must be harnessed and exploited to your benefit or you will find yourself shipwrecked.

Ultimately, tacking is accomplished by using two kinds of resistance—the wind (aerodynamics) and the water (hydrodynamics)—against one another so that the path of least resistance becomes forward, into the wind, rather than backward, or with the wind. Clever manipulation of the two in respect to one another enables sailors to travel in any direction by generating an additional source of lift from the water. The combination of the aerodynamic force from the sails and the hydrodynamic force from the keel gives you the power to navigate in almost any condition.

> *Your core beliefs may not be visible on the surface, but they nonetheless affect your progress and direction in life.*

Think of your trials as a gift from the hands of God that squeeze you from all sides and catapult you on to a new course. They come to help you discover who you really are so that you can live with renewed integrity (being true to the real you) and provide you with an opportunity to establish your credibility as a problem solver. Problems come so that you can have a testimony of overcoming. Personal experience is the only way to build your credibility as well as your capacity to do more.

You don't know the stuff you are made of until you are met with a challenge. Setting sail toward a desired port of call, or destination, is the first step to accomplishing your goals. Deciding where you want to end up and what you want to accomplish is paramount to navigating the seas of life. This can't be done without skill. So, before you set sail, you've got to know what kind of sailing vessel you are. You have to understand how to harness the wind by trimming the sail, as well as how to keep the keel steady and headed on course. Then you can command the crew—your gifts, talents, skills, and abilities—in order to maintain an "even keel." The crew is often referred to as the "live or moveable ballast" used to balance or "right the ship." Facing your problems starts with acknowledging you are not on an "even keel."

> *You don't know the stuff you are made of until you meet with a challenge.*

When have you felt "off keel"? How can you reposition your sails, rudder, and crew to take advantage of the winds you're currently facing? List some of the winds you're feeling blow against your purpose, hopes, and dreams, both externally and internally. Consider how you might better leverage them to propel you forward.

> *It is not the ship so much as the skillful sailing that assures the prosperous voyage.*
> —GEORGE WILLIAM CURTIS

Facet Six: INSPIRE

LEAD CHANGE

Leadership is unlocking people's potential to become better.
—BILL BRADLEY

Basketball legend Bill Bradley once said, "Sports is a metaphor for overcoming obstacles and achieving against great odds"—which is why he also asserted, "Athletes, in times of difficulty, can be important role models." As we discussed in the last chapter, life's complications strengthen your character, bolster your credibility, and build your capacity. As your capacity expands, so does your influence. You become a role model and that makes you a leader, whether you had intended to be one or not. This puts you in a position to help unlock the potential in others as they learn to overcome their own obstacles and "achieve against great odds." Great odds make for great achievers.

An individual will not know the gifts and talents that lie dormant within them unless something forces them into the light.

Life's complications strengthen your character, bolster your credibility, and build your capacity.

Every single person is a diamond in the rough. You may be tempted to look at what is wrong with a person and focus on their flaws, but a diamond with a flaw is more valuable than a perfect lump of coal. You are no different. We are all works in progress, but those who see the potential in themselves and others will progress the most. Learn to see the potential in your problems, and then help others see the valuable insights hidden in their challenges as well.

PROBLEMS PROPEL US INTO NEW REALMS OF INNOVATION, SUCCESS, AND PROSPERITY

Every problem demands a solution; every question cries for an answer. The more difficult the problem or complicated the question, the more compelled and clever we will be in our search for the answer. Think for a moment of the stories of some of the greatest problem solvers of all time: Albert Einstein, Thomas Edison, Marie Curie, Wilber and Orville Wright, Alexander Graham Bell, Clara Barton, Martin Luther King Jr., Mahatma Gandhi, Nelson Mandela, and Steve Jobs, just to name a few. The problems they faced were some of the most challenging the world has known, yet because they tackled them—even though they didn't always tackle them successfully—their names will never be forgotten.

Overcoming life's challenges forces unexpressed potential to surface from deep within you. Problems will shine divine spotlights on hidden possibilities that have been dormant. Problems not only cause the brilliant luster of your own gifts to shine, but they bring out the brilliance of a community or team—even a nation—in times of crisis.

PROBLEMS SHAPE GREAT LEADERS

President Barack Obama made history the day he became the first man of color to become president of the United States of America. He is quoted as saying:

> Making your mark in the world is hard. If it were easy, everybody would do it. But it takes patience, it takes

commitment, and it comes with plenty of failure along the way. The real test is not whether you avoid this failure, because you won't. It is whether you let it harden you or shame you into inaction; whether you learn from it, or whether you choose to persevere.[1]

I have discovered that there is no real security in comfort or remaining complacent. There is no real benefit in staying with things or in situations that no longer hold meaning or value, or that are not making a positive impact. Let God open new doors of opportunities—or should we say problems—that will allow you to express your purpose and broadcast the strength of your character to the world around you.

> *Overcoming life's challenges forces unexpressed potential to surface.*

True empowerment comes when you move toward a desired change or a new goal that makes a difference beyond yourself as an individual, no matter how small the action or contribution. It is the moving out from your comfort zone into the unknown that requires the most courage.

"What if I fail?" you might be asking. I would ask you, "What if you do?" Leaders keep moving even with past failures close on their heels and the potential of new ones continually underfoot—each one is just another stepping-stone to ultimate triumph.

Failure gives relevance and significance to success, even though failure and success exist at opposite ends of the same continuum. Keep pushing the envelope. Stand up for what is right. Do what is proper, not only for yourself but also for the people around you.

Persevering in spite of your failures is important. Failure, in fact, is the only way humankind has been able to progress. Someone tried something new and failed, but got back in the saddle and tried again and again until they succeeded. Successful people are just getting started when others are ready to quit. Leaders are those willing to try that one additional time that others are not.

When I think of tenacity, I'm reminded of people like the Wright brothers and Thomas Edison. It has been noted that Edison once remarked, "I have not failed. I've just found 10,000 ways that won't work." Had he stopped after his first failed attempt—or 999th—we might still be sitting in dark houses at night struggling to read by candlelight. Leaders, as Winston Churchill so famously said, "Never, never, never, never give up."

As a leader, you will be challenged on every front. You will have to withstand the cruel winds of controversy and criticism. You will have to fight your own inner voice that tells you to quit or to settle for the status quo. It will take courage—courage to move out of your comfort zone of conformity and compromise. Martin Luther King Jr. stated, "The ultimate measure of a man is not where he stands in moments of comfort and convenience, but where he stands at times of challenge and controversy."

> *We need leaders who have the courage to show the way and lead by example.*

In our generation, we need leaders who have the courage to show the way and lead by example. I agree with Vince Lombardi when he stated, "Leaders aren't born, they are made. And they are made just like anything else, through hard work"—and with Lee Iacocca who observed, "Leadership is forged in times of crisis."[2]

During my many visits to Africa, I became familiar with the African saying, "No shaking!" This means, "Take courage, and dare to make your mark!" Lead in your industry, lead in your community, lead in your home, lead in your schools and universities, lead amongst your peers, lead amongst your competitors. In whatever you do, lead! The world awaits your gift of leadership.

> *Leadership is scarce because few people are willing to go through the discomfort required to lead. This scarcity makes leadership valuable.*[3]
> —SETH GODIN

PART TWO:

COLOR

THE PROSPERING POWER OF PERSPECTIVE

Some people grumble that roses have thorns;
I am grateful that thorns have roses.
—ALPHONSE KARR

Everything we see is a perspective, not the truth.
—MARCUS AURELIUS

Facts are just what there aren't, there
are only interpretations.[1]
—FRIEDRICH NIETZSCHE

Facet Seven: ADJUST

RECOLOR YOUR WORLD

Most folks are about as happy as they
make their minds up to be.
—ABRAHAM LINCOLN

How do you see your life? Do you see your glass as half empty or half full? That particular metaphor reminds me of the difference between the concepts of fate versus destiny. Although I don't believe in fate, most people see fate as a product of the circumstances they have been born into or the "hand" they have been dealt in life. And, if you are like most of the world's population, you could liken it to the glass being half empty. Destiny, on the other hand, is a matter of choice—you can choose to change your circumstances *if* you're willing to see your glass as half full. In fact, if you are among those who are determined to fulfill their destiny in spite of their background or current state of affairs, you will have to learn the art of perspective.

Abraham Lincoln had quite a lot to say about the topic of perspective. He wisely puts forth, "We can complain because rose bushes have thorns, or we can rejoice because thorn bushes have roses." Either way, it is a matter of choice and perspective. Depending on what you choose to see, you will either have a rose bush or a thorn bush. So which would you prefer? If you want to prosper in life, learn to harness the power of perspective. If you want roses, learn to see roses. Perspective is a powerful force, and if you learn to command it well you will certainly outshine the average gemstone.

In talking about the concept of color as it relates to a diamond, the more clear the stone is, the better. We're after a colorless transparency—no hue or tint or hint of color. So what about seeing roses—our rose-colored glasses? What we see and how we're seen are very different things. In terms of how others see us, we must be perfectly clear, which means we must be transparently honest. Say what you mean and mean what you say—no "putting on airs" or artificial façades that tarnish your authenticity, which only speaks of being double-minded. James wrote that he who is double-minded is *"unstable in all his ways."*[1]

If you want to prosper in life, learn to harness the power of perspective.

Just as a diamond is more highly valued when it is devoid of color—transparently clear—so are we more potent when we're authentic and void of pretense. This requires a certain degree of vulnerability. Author Stephen Russell writes that, "Vulnerability is the only authentic state." He goes on to explain:

> Being vulnerable means being open, for wounding, but also for pleasure. Being open to the wounds of life means also being open to the bounty and beauty. Don't mask or deny your vulnerability: It is your greatest asset. Be vulnerable; quake and shake in your boots with it. The new goodness that is coming to you in the form of people, situations, and things can only come to you when you are vulnerable.[2]

In this section we'll be focusing on keeping a clear, unbiased perspective in the way we view life, and the circumstances of life. As with a diamond, we are looking for a colorless hue, which will require us to be vulnerable. As Mr. Russell stated above, vulnerability is your greatest asset, strengthening and freeing you to be open about who you are and what you stand for. It will enable you to walk with greater integrity. So keep a positive perspective, always exercising your inherent power to choose while remaining true to your values, vision, and what uniquely drives you. You are all called to be genuine with yourself and others because inauthenticity will tint people's perspective of you.

Make up your mind about how you will choose to live. Choose to see the good in people and to see abundance and beauty around you, as well as *within* you—your authentic, abundant goodness. You are enough even in the rough. You can be unpolished, but under what may be a rough exterior, you are solid and clear. Your color—or transparent quality—has already been determined. As with a rough diamond, your interior remains unchanged. You are already made perfect in substance and form at your core.[3]

Therefore, be willing to practice vulnerability to maintain that purity and transparency that is so highly valued. I've heard it said, "Genuine people don't come around too often. If you find someone real enough to stay true, keep them close." Make up your mind to be genuine— not only will you be genuinely happier,

> *Don't allow inauthenticity to stain your internal sense of integrity.*

but so will the people around you. It will free everyone to relax and step out from behind the curtain. In fact, just throw open all the curtains and let the light in! Where there is light, there is also liberty.[4]

Founder and president of the Children's Defense Fund, Marian Wright Edelman, wisely advised, "Learn to be quiet enough to hear the genuine within yourself so that you can hear it in others." Don't allow inauthenticity to stain your internal sense of integrity. How true, or truthful, you are with yourself will determine how you see other people and, of course, how they see you. People will sense when you are being disingenuous, pretentious, or insincere. Honestly examine whether you are in the habit of erecting a "people pleasing" façade or are ever tempted to be less than authentic by hiding behind a veneer of invulnerability.

More than anything else, be honest. How does that make you feel? More like a rose bush or a thorn bush? Does it predispose you to seeing the glass half empty or half full? Changing your perspective will add value to the clarity of your life.

There is something in every one of you that waits
and listens for the sound of the genuine in yourself.
...It is the only true guide you will ever have.
...And if you cannot hear it, you will all of your life
spend your days on the ends of strings
that somebody else pulls.[5]
—HOWARD THURMAN

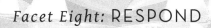

Facet Eight: RESPOND

ANSWER THE CALL

You have God-blessed eyes—eyes that see!
And God-blessed ears—ears that hear![1]
—JESUS

Problems, adversities, challenges, loss, and opposition are inescapable components of life. They are as certain as death and taxes. But I have a secret to tell you: spending your life running from such things is not only useless, but it is also counterproductive. Joy in life doesn't come from living a problem-free, blissful, uneventful existence—because where there are no obstacles, there are no triumphs and there is no story to tell. No, the truth of the matter is that joy in life comes from facing problems and in finding a way to overcome and solve them.

Problems, as we have seen, are opportunities in disguise. God doesn't allow them to come into our lives as a punishment for living in a fallen world. He allows them so that we can grow through conquering them. This is the essence of the promise given by Paul:

> *We know that all things work together for good to those who*
> *love God, to those who are the called according to His purpose.*

...Yet in all these things we are more than conquerors through Him who loved us.[2]

So what then is the purpose of the problems we encounter throughout our lives? Is it not to awaken the sleeping oak that lies within the acorn? Is it not to expose the diamond obscured in its sooty carbon casing? Is it not to announce the emergence of the next champion who will slay the new giant? Is it not an urgent, necessary call to action—a calling forth of unused energy, unexpressed gifts, hidden potential, slumbering intelligence, innate abilities, innovations, ideas, and inventions yet to be roused? Is it not to reveal to us the true nature of our souls and the value of our lives? Is it not a divine announcement that prosperity and progress are just around the corner if we would only stand up and be the person God has called each of us to be?

> *Where there are no obstacles, there are no triumphs.*

STEP THROUGH THE DOOR

If appreciated for their intrinsic value, problems can be viewed as doors of opportunity opening into new realms of possibility. How so? Because they demand the expression and employment of latent potential—spiritual, mental, and emotional resources— gifts, talents, and abilities that we might never have known we possessed were it not for the emergence of a specific problem. Problems call for the development of a deeper spiritual insight, broader mental discipline, and greater inner fortitude.

It has been said, "No problem can be solved from the same level of consciousness that created it."[3] Problems also challenge us at our core because they expose our values, veracity, and valor. They cause us to ask, "Do I have what is necessary to connect with my truest identity—to accomplish my goals and realize my potential?"

Problems call you to the place of your greatest personal power—for in overcoming challenges, you move closer to realizing your destiny. They usher you into realms of greater responsibility, accountability, and authority, which is what makes life so dynamic, thrilling, rewarding, and challenging all at the same time. Every challenge will lead you closer to what God placed you on the earth to accomplish. Therefore, every challenge you encounter must be responded to thoughtfully and strategically.

History is not made in comfort and ease. It is made by those who, against seemingly insurmountable odds, push the envelope, defy the status quo, and go against the grain; those who through conviction and courage emerge out of their greatest challenges as innovators, trailblazers, overcomers, artistic masters, and industry leaders. They are the individuals who help us view every negative event we experience as a milestone marker and destiny changer—not only for ourselves but potentially for the entire world. History is made in seconds—those critical moments that determine the outcome of a decision and the trajectory of our future. These are defining moments. These are moments that have the power to turn otherwise uneventful moments into history-making and watershed moments—moments that change the course of our collective lives.

Problems call you to the place of your greatest personal power.

HOLD YOUR POSITION

As you look back throughout history, in every era you will find characters whose lives seem strangely similar to your own. Their stories are stories of challenge, change, courage, and, if they made a difference in the end, triumph. Many, in their greatest hour, fell flat on their faces in an attempt to make sense out of life, while others used those same obstacles as stepping-stones to something greater. Their times were riddled with triumphs and tragedies.

Though it may seem counterintuitive, James the apostle was right when he said, *"Count it all joy when you fall into various trials,"*[4] for it is through trials and tests that we grow and create change. Think about when you were in school—tests weren't given to trip you up so your teacher could give you a bad grade (although that might have seemed the case). Rather, tests were administered to help you learn and grow. Once you passed, you moved on to the next class, level, or grade. But if you failed, you risked repeating the same lesson again and again until you mastered it. The same is true in life. Problems, trials, impasses, and complications are in our lives to enlarge our capacity—if we don't have the capacity to work through the challenges we currently face, we will have to repeat them until we have grown in our ability to handle more. God is always in the process of maturing you, completing the good work He began in you the day you were conceived.

As you consider your situation today, no matter what lies before you, don't be seduced into believing that somehow you will be exempt from the obstacles and problems that come with being human. Life itself is experienced in seasons—highs and lows, good days and not so good days, light and dark, joy and sorrow, exaltation and humiliation, success and failure, gain and loss. Forget about self-confidence and self-esteem—they're overrated and often fail us when challenges are at their height.

God is always in the process of maturing you—completing the good work He began in you the day you were conceived.

Cultivate, instead, God-confidence. See yourself as God sees you. Lean on Him. Rely on Him. Learn to trust and delight in Him, and *"lean not on your own understanding."*[5]

You are not alone when it comes to feeling alone in your situation, as if no one else could possibly understand. It may feel that way now, but it is not the truth. No test or temptation that comes your way is beyond what others have already faced, though it may look different in this decade than it looked in the past, or in one part of the world than in another. However, God remains constant through any distance of time or geography. He is no more perplexed by the twenty-first century than He was by the first, or by the problems facing Southeast Asia than those facing southern California. All you need to remember is that your God is faithful, He will never let you down, He'll never let you be tested beyond what you can handle, and He'll always be there to see you through, just as His Word promises:

> *No test or temptation that comes your way is beyond the course of what others have had to face. All you need to remember is that God will never let you down; He'll never let you be pushed past your limit; He'll always be there to help you come through it.*[6]

SEE YOURSELF FINISHING STRONG

Tests and trials come to help you build inner fortitude, moral strength, rock-solid faith, and unshakable character. Building these characteristics is like building physical muscles—they must be broken down through repetition and resistance before they can be built back up again. They must be stretched and stressed if they are to grow stronger.

You are what you repeatedly do. Therefore, you are where you are today, and you have what you have today, based on your habits. Taking personal responsibility for where you are is not the easiest thing to do. Most of us would prefer pointing at others or at circumstances for why our lives are the way they are. We cry, "I am a victim," or "Life is unfair," or "No one will help me!" We look at the broken pieces of our aspirations from a broken place and wonder what happened. I'll tell you what happened: You met a challenge, and rather than conquering it and gaining strength through the experience, you let it conquer you. But I have good news for you: Past defeat has no bearing on your future success other than propelling you closer to it.

Ernest Hemingway once said, "The world breaks everyone, and afterward many are stronger at the broken places."[7] What doesn't kill you *can* indeed make you stronger—it depends on how you respond. Will you embrace the opportunity to grow through a setback or shrink back and do nothing other than complain? Could things be the way they are because you are the way you are? What one thing can you change that might change everything?

You can change your mind. You can change your attitude. You can change the way you think and talk about your life starting right now. Don't wait until everything looks or feels how you want it to. Make a choice. It is this sole decision—or *soul* decision—that can turn any tragedy into a triumph.

Every problem requires a response—a particular action or reaction. The weak react, but the strong *pro*-act. Problems don't happen to them; they happen to problems. They have a plan that plots out what to do about the unexpected before it even arrives. The strong respond according to conviction rather than emotion. They never lose sight of what they value most. They are able to assess why they ended up where they are and readjust in order to go where they want to be. They remain clear and uncompromising about who they are and where they're headed.

> *Past defeat has no bearing on your future success other than propelling you closer to it!*

The line has to be drawn, and you must decide on which side you will live—whether you will live an empowered life or an impotent life. I believe that we all have power but many of us give it away to things, circumstances, and people, claiming we have no control over our own choices, because somehow "life just happens." However, as Victor Frankl suggested in his classic book *Man's Search for Meaning*, forces beyond our control can take away everything we possess except one thing, our freedom to choose how we will respond. "In some way," said Frankl, "suffering ceases to be suffering at the moment it finds a meaning."[8]

For what then matters is to bear witness to the uniquely human potential at its best, which is to transform a personal tragedy into a triumph, to turn one's predicament into a human achievement.[9]

"It is not about what we expect from life, but rather about what life expects from us," he further postulates, adding that we should "stop asking about the meaning of life, and instead to think of ourselves as those who were being questioned by life—daily and hourly...taking the responsibility to find the right answer to its problems and to fulfill the tasks which it constantly sets for each individual."[10]

> *Fate is what happens to you; destiny is what you choose to do in spite of it.*

Every day you have choices to make. You, and you alone, must decide whether you will allow outside forces to control your life, or whether you will take your personal power back and *decide* to be a victor rather than a victim. Fate is what happens to you; destiny is what you choose to do in spite of it. The choice belongs to no one else but you.

So do not throw away your confidence;
it will be richly rewarded.
You need to persevere so that when you
have done the will of God,
you will receive what He has promised.[11]

Facet Nine: DEFINE

REMOVE THE CONFUSION

If we had no winter, the spring would not be so pleasant;
if we did not sometimes taste of adversity,
prosperity would not be so welcome.
—ANNE BRADSTREET

Without obstacles there would be no breakthroughs, and without challenges there would be no advancement, no unfolding of destiny, and no progress. Universal stagnation would prevail. Hope would perish. Humanity would flounder in dark obscurity while books, inventions, medical breakthroughs, musical scores, and the like remained buried in the graveyard of broken dreams and hidden in the shadow of unrealized potential.

It has been said, "Even as a gem cannot be polished without friction, a person can never be perfected without trials." You may be asking, like I often do, "When does the polishing come to an end?" The answer is that it comes to an end when your truest identity is drawn out of you.

Sometimes cooperation is more powerful than comprehension. I retrospectively ponder the road that has brought me to the place I am currently in and see the wisdom of God through it all. But as I was making the journey, there were many days that nothing made sense. And so it will be with you. Sometimes you can't make sense out of life. But rest assured in this: All things will eventually work together for your good. Trust the loving hands of your heavenly Father—the Potter molding and making you into a vessel of honor fit for His use.[1] One day your wounds will become your wisdom and your test your testimony.

Every crisis is an opportunity to build character, to forge the inner strength to go the distance and follow your dreams. Charles de Gaulle said that when we are "faced with crisis, the man of character falls back on himself. He imposes his own stamp of action, takes responsibility for it, and makes it his own." After all, you have been created in the image of God, and like Him you have the power to make choices. You have the ability to change fate by activating your faith not only in God but also in the person He created you to be.

> *You have the ability to change fate by activating your faith not only in God but also in the person He created you to be.*

Abraham Lincoln, the sixteenth president of the United States, rose to prominence from humble beginnings. This self-taught prairie lawyer born in a log cabin embodied the extraordinary transitional leadership that overcame the greatest moral challenge to democracy the United States of America has ever faced: the issue of slavery and the right of states to withdraw if they disagreed with the majority. Lincoln was born into a world where slavery was justified by many, upheld as being constitutionally legal and biblically acceptable. Lincoln, however, contended that it was unethical, absurd, and a "great moral wrong," and that no justification could be made for relegating another human being to the status of "property," while at the same time proclaiming the United States as "the land of the free."

Although he believed in the rule of law and the tenets contained within the Constitution, it is hard for me to imagine the inner turmoil Lincoln must have felt as he tackled the issue of slavery in his day. In his first inaugural address, he called upon the "chords of memory stretching from every battlefield and patriot grave to every human heart," hoping that as a nation we would be guided by the "better angels of our nature." In this I believe he was referring to the moral compass of social justice and the virtue of equality espoused by the Declaration of Independence relative to "life, liberty, and the pursuit of happiness" *for all.*

The Civil War, the deadliest war in American history, would have broken the will of most people, but Lincoln never gave up or gave in. This was his destiny—the very crucible that defined his greatness and revealed the brilliance of his character. He never buckled under criticism. Instead, he distinguished himself as a true fighter, one whose respect for humanity and desire for unity allowed him no other option than to fight until he achieved victory.

He exhorted his countrymen throughout the gruesome nights of conflict between the North and South and the long days of hardship endured by his beloved nation. In spite of the challenges and criticism, he has gone down as America's greatest president and the quintessential transformational leader. He left an indelible mark forever

> Are you willing to step out of your comfort zone to be the world-changer God intended for you to become?

etched into the marble of history because he stood on the side of unity and freedom through the toughest war America ever faced. You must face your battles with as much resolution, determined never to give in to the external forces of compromise.

HOW WILL YOU FACE YOUR BATTLES?

Today we are faced with our own challenging battles. We are in the middle of fighting some of the greatest wars this generation has ever seen, with no demilitarized zones. There is a war on drugs and terrorism, corruption, homelessness, global warming, domestic violence, poverty, human trafficking, child soldiers, racism, and religious persecution, just to name those at the top of the list. Today's world is increasingly becoming one big global village—issues that used to seem a world away are now impossible to ignore.

Because of their scope, these global issues are overwhelming, even for the most sophisticated governments. If we are to turn these trends around, we need all hands on deck—my hands and your hands. We need a global vision for global results in dismantling international syndicates and the multitudes of acquiescing mindsets that are either part of the problem or believe nothing can be done. Even as the world remembers Abraham Lincoln, may the world one day remember you for your dedication and commitment, and your resolve and courage to address the issues pressing hardest on your heart. You can make a difference when you take a stand—when you become adamant about finding your voice and speaking up for what you believe.

What national or international challenge takes your breath away every time you hear about it? Could it be that the thing weighing heaviest on your heart is God putting His thumb on the scale of your perceptions? Is it possible this passion stirs within you for a reason—for a time such as this? Is it because God is stirring you up for greatness? Is it because the thing that breaks your heart is breaking God's heart? Are you willing to step out of your comfort zone to be the world-changer God intended for you to become?

People who dread trials or circumvent difficulties will never fully realize their potential. The only ones who will are those who fight through challenges with an indomitable spirit and those who resign themselves to build character by exploring the depth of their truest nature when times seem at their worst. It will be those who mine and refine the courage that God has placed at the very core of their beings. Will you be the one within your generation who allows Him to temper and empower you to fight to victory the arduous struggle before you?

THE REAL PROBLEM

We can gain personal revelation of how trials, temptations, and challenges bring the best out of countries, organizations, families, and businesses in crisis if we perceive them as opportunities for growth and catalysts for development and progress. Lydia M. Child said, "Every man deems that he has precisely the trials and temptations which are the hardest of all others for him to bear; but they are so, simply because they are the very ones he most needs."[2] The problems we face are not usually the real problem. The real problem exists with our perception of those problems.

Problems are portals. To some, problems are perceived as barriers and obstacles; to others, they are seen as either an exit or an entrance. I believe they are revolving doors. You have three options when you come to a revolving door:

1. You can stay in the 360-degree circular movement of the door, going around and around in a state of perpetual confusion.

2. You can make the 360-degree revolution in the door and exit at the same spot you entered, staying in the same condition and predicament you were in when you started.

3. You can exit on the other side and arrive in an entirely new place.

Which do you choose? I encourage you to embrace the door of opportunity hidden within problems for your own growth, change, evolution, development, and progress. If you are confronted with obstacles, trials, and tribulations, it means you have reached the end of some particular state of being, some predicament of immaturity, some condition of stagnation, some expression of irresponsibility, some stronghold of oppression, or are ready to transition out of a place you have outgrown. Problems are a call to the next level.

When you face a test or a trial, you are suddenly called upon to summon all resources—acumen, energies, gifts, abilities, and intelligence—in order to be extricated from one level of life to the next. Think of it as an "exit exam" before graduating to whatever is next for you. Problems challenge you to find new ways of doing business, better ways to conduct your affairs, or healthier routes to desired success and prosperity. They will test your systems and practices and show you weaknesses that need to be corrected, and, if you are courageous enough to confront them, those things that may have appeared meant for evil will instead be turned to your good.

> *With each new challenge, you have a new opportunity to remove the confusion and respond differently.*

A problem can be a path that will lead you to the discovery of a power and potential you never knew you possessed. Overcoming setbacks and roadblocks will produce greater freedom, enlarging the scope of your world—it will, as Jabez prayed, "enlarge your territory"[3]—and it will give you a context and scope beyond your personal possessions, acquisitions, and achievements. Napoleon Hill described it this way: "Every adversity brings with it the seed of an equivalent advantage."[4] Sometimes it is hard to embrace this as truth because of the unpleasantness and discomfort of facing some problems, but then this is why we get stuck in cycles of pain. It is only when we embrace the truth that we are set free.[5]

Psychologist Gordon Allport, famous for his "personal traits" theory of personality, was amazed at how two different people could face basically the same circumstances but have completely different reactions to them. As he explained it, "The same heat that melts the butter, hardens the egg."[6] Where one person melts when confronted with a problem, the other hardens their resolve to push through to victory.

Which type of person will you be? You may have a predisposition to react one way or the other, but with each new challenge you have a new opportunity to remove the confusion and respond differently. Will you be the chicken who in his confusion proclaimed, "The sky is falling!" or the egg containing the seed of new possibilities?

So much of life is how we react to what we experience.
We cannot control everything that happens to us,
but we can control our choices in response.
Because we see various perspectives,
we also visualize creative solutions.
You are now more powerful than ever.[7]
—DR. KEVIN SNYDER

MAKE THE VITAL CHOICE

I look to the future, because that's where
I'm going to spend the rest of my life.
—GEORGE BURNS

I believe that any time you encounter a problem or a point of impasse, a place where you are stuck and not sure how to go on, there are only three possible reactions: You can cower, conform, or create. You can cower and try to ignore the problem, you can conform to the status quo, or you can choose to create something new. The choice is up to you.

How you choose to respond will determine the outcome. The circumstances won't determine the outcome; it is the choices you make as a result of the circumstances that will either propel you forward or pull you back. Every time you encounter a difficulty, you have a vital choice to make when it comes to your future.

DON'T CAVE UNDER PRESSURE

Your first option is always to quit, to capitulate, to be the victim who points their finger at some other culprit, passes the buck, or buckles under the pressure and accepts defeat. By playing the blame game and not taking responsibility, you allow external factors to determine whether you succeed or fail. If you let someone else solve the problem for you, you give away your personal power to tackle the issue yourself and control the outcome. You can certainly ask for help, but that doesn't mean you should avoid taking ownership and contributing to your own growth and success. Every impasse affords you the opportunity to become stronger, braver, and wiser—if rather than turning and running from it, you engage and learn from it, listen and grow through the advice of others, and position yourself to help others escape from the same dilemmas. The option you choose will depend on your perspective.

If there is anyone who is an example of accepting and giving help in the right way, it is Dave Ramsey. Charismatic and ambitious, Dave Ramsey learned early how foolish it can be to live beyond your means when easy credit is made available everywhere. When the money in his real estate business was flowing well, he was on top of the world, but when he made some "stupid, risky mistakes," as he puts it, everything turned upside down. Suddenly he had more and more month left after his paycheck was spent, and no way to pay back what he had borrowed. This forced him to accept the legal protection that bankruptcy offers. It was a painful experience.

Every time you encounter a difficulty you have a vital choice to make when it comes to your future.

Humbling himself, he asked the difficult questions and learned from the process, and when he emerged, he determined to help others never have to face what he had gone through.

Out of his experience, Dave carefully studied what had happened to him, read extensively about financial management (learning things he had never been taught in college finance), and talked to successful people about how they handled money. He compiled this material and his own experiences into a class for others facing bankruptcy. That led to books and a tape series about how to manage money and build wealth while living a godly, generous life.[1] He was invited to host a talk radio show where people could call in and ask questions about money. This turned into his widely acclaimed Financial Peace University, which teaches people what they need to know not only to avoid bankruptcy, but also how to save, pay for their children's college educations, retire well, and pass on wealth and wisdom to their children and their grandchildren. As further evidence of what he had learned, Dave even went back and paid off the balances on the debts that had been forgiven when he filed bankruptcy—something he was not required by law to do, but that he did out of the conviction of his heart.

Dave Ramsey stood on the brink of a financial cliff—one that sets many back for a lifetime—but he took bankruptcy and failure and turned them into a ministry that has kept over a million and a half people from being forced over the edge as he was. He failed and accepted help, but he never quit. He engaged, learned, and now teaches others to succeed where he had stumbled. Facing your problems doesn't always mean you come out unscathed, but if you do it right, you will emerge stronger and better on the other side.

> *Those who choose to create solutions rather than avoid problems are the way-makers.*

THE VALLEY OF CONFORMITY

The second thing you can do when you face an impasse or problem is to *conform*. In other words, you do what everyone else is doing. You look around and if everyone else is sticking their head in the sand, you stick your head in the sand too; if everyone is talking about an issue yet doing nothing, you talk about the issue just as passionately while also doing nothing; if they throw a little money at it hoping that will ease their conscience, you do the same thing. You don't really engage; you just go along with the crowd. You don't confront the problem; you accept it and try to get along like everyone else.

Both quitting and conforming are defeatist attitudes that will keep you from growing. People with such attitudes shun responsibility and refuse to take up the issue at hand. They play it safe, always doing the same and getting the same. They dumb themselves down, remaining complacent, weak, and ineffective.

But there is always another choice. The third option is to choose to *create* your way out of, or through, the impasse. Those who choose to create solutions rather than avoid problems are the way-makers. They are the inventors, innovators, teachers, and reconcilers. They are the chart toppers, award winners, and world-hangers. They are the ones who make things better for everyone around them. Those who choose to be creators rather than conformers make all the difference in the world.

CHOOSE YOUR THOUGHTS WISELY

When facing a hardship, learn to tap into the strength-giving catalysts of faith, love, and hope, for these three forces will empower you to persevere. In fact, they are the three most powerful of all human virtues and will give you the strength to overcome every vice. I believe that they are also God's cure-all for life and living. Overdose, and the only side effects you will experience will be peace, prosperity, happiness, and joy. The greater the dosage, the more dynamic and meaningful your life will be. When these three virtues are braided together, they instantly penetrate your subconscious mind, demolishing doubt and negativity. Your own mind, will, and emotions hold the key to success because every thought it produces draws to you spiritual resources that can overcome physical experiences, circumstances, or barriers.

If you, by faith, can see victory in spite of your circumstances, and if you can challenge yourself to hold loving thoughts in your mind and hope for a favorable outcome, no matter how obstinate your condition, you will be on the path to seeing incredible things manifested in your life and in the world around you. Repeat over and over again, "With God nothing is impossible. Neither my condition nor situation is too hard for God. Every day and in every way my life gets better and better."[2]

When facing a problem, never allow doubt, hatred, fear, or disappointment to invade your soul or settle in your subconscious. These negative emotions, when mixed together, have the opposite effect of faith, hope, and love. If you let them, they will exacerbate the original problem by drawing you into a cycle of negativity, helplessness, hopelessness, and defeat.

> *Faith, hope, and love form an elixir, so that when they are blended together, they become the catalyst for happy and healthy living.*

Faith, hope, and love form an elixir, so that when they are blended together, they become the catalyst for happy and healthy living. Mixed with a daily dose of faith confession and believing prayer, the subconscious mind instantly operates on a higher frequency, tapping into a spiritual force that becomes fuel to propel you into a dynamic state of prosperity and well-being. Your only limitations are those you construct in your own mind through unbelief, fear, and despair. Never allow yourself to utter the words, "I'm afraid" or "I can't" or "I'm sick and tired," because these are thoughts and statements you don't want taking root in your mind. Instead, make this your mantra: "Every day, in every way, I am getting better, growing stronger, and becoming wiser."

Fight fear as an unarmed, impotent enemy standing between you and your dreams. Replace unbelief with the thought, "All things are possible," because with God all things truly are possible.[3] If there is one thing you can change that will change everything, it is the way you perceive and address your problems. Don't quit or conform—choose to create a better life for yourself and those you love.

There are two primary choices in life:
To accept conditions as they exist,
or accept responsibility for changing them.[4]
—DENIS WAITLEY

PLANT SEEDS OF SOLUTION

Every problem has in it the seeds of its own solution.
If you don't have any problems, you don't get any seeds.
—NORMAN VINCENT PEALE

W hat is, is," is a maxim worth examining. Circumstances do happen and bad things do exist, but our challenge is in how we face outward realities and adjust our mindsets, thoughts, and paradigms so we can learn new strategies for creating solutions. Only then are we challenged to go within and pull from our spiritual storehouses the potential that was planted there before we were even conceived.[1] These hidden resources must be awakened. As you accept the challenge to surmount whatever obstacles you face through prayer and the enabling power of the Spirit of God, you will discover that God has already wired you to overcome and achieve success.

In fact, God may be using His sovereign power over a situation or circumstance to reveal the fortitude and creativity lying dormant within you. Just as the majestic oak tree is awakened from out of the tiny acorn through heat and pressure, so is your own majesty. It is the heat of the trial and the pressure to respond that exposes and germinates the seeds of greatness within you.

In good times and bad, you will be challenged to find the strength to pray, to trust God, and to believe. This takes discipline, which is what will make you powerful. Success only happens when the discipline of preparation meets the possibility of an opportunity—opportunities most often hidden within the seeds of your most difficult problems.

If you persist beyond that tipping point of giving up or giving in, you will build the spiritual muscles and mental fortitude to overcome any present or future challenge. This is the state where the noble become nobler and the kind more compassionate; a state where your problem-solving skills flow, the champion within emerges, and the inventor, the genius, and the general receive strategies to turn the tide in the heat of battle. With the necessary insight, foresight, and oversight, you can leverage any obstacle to your advantage.

> *It is the heat of the trial and the pressure to respond that exposes and germinates the seeds of greatness within you.*

SOW IN HUMILITY, REAP IN HONOR

When you pay attention to the way you repeatedly respond to situations and conditions, you will learn to make adjustments. The key is humble circumspection. To be honest with your self requires humility. No matter how tightly you are bound to your current condition, you can break free if you are willing to surrender your agenda and submit to God's better plan. Even if you find yourself entangled in unhealthy relationships, debt, addiction, or questionable activities, you can always rediscover who you are, recover your strength of character, and restore your integrity, honor, and dignity. Shame, anger, resentment, and hurt can eventually give way to peace, joy, and right living. This is what salvation is all about. Even if you find yourself walking through the valley of the shadow of death, you are to fear no evil, for God is with you.[2] He has not abandoned you nor left you in an orphaned state.[3] He is your heavenly Father, and like the father in the story of the prodigal son, He is waiting for you to find your way home.[4]

Even in the midst of the pain born out of hardships and misfortunes, you can discover your true self and travel the path that leads you back to meaning, fulfillment, and purpose. You only have to ask God to help you retrace your steps (and as a leader or policy maker, you can use the same strategy to pull your organization, corporation, government, or nation out of its crisis as well), and you will soon discern where you made a wrong turn, where a little more sensitivity to the prompting of the Spirit of God or a little more caution, prudence, economy, or self-denial would have saved you from your present circumstances. You will notice step by step how a clearer mind and keener judgment would have enabled you to take an altogether different and truer course, positioning and establishing you in a place of greater authenticity and power. It is never too late to make a course correction.

Learning to sow to the Spirit (the eternal) rather than the flesh (things temporal or that which gives immediate gratification) is the first step in planting seeds of solution and success in your life. It is the most significant investment you can make that will yield the most returns, even beyond what you can ask or imagine.[5] It is the primary thing—the principal principle—that will prosper everything you do, but more importantly it will help you turn setbacks into comebacks. It is the effective working of His mighty power[6] that completes the good work He has begun, sprouts the seeds of potential He has sown, and reveals the diamond forged in the crucibles of your hardships and heartaches.

Invest yourself in seeking God, serving others, and giving generously, and you will build a portfolio—a solid platform—a safety net that will protect and prosper you. As Paul instructed the Galatians:

What a person plants, he will harvest. The person who plants selfishness, ignoring the needs of others—ignoring God!—harvests a crop of weeds. All he'll have to show for his life is weeds! But the one who plants in response to God, letting God's Spirit do the growth work in him, harvests a crop of real life, eternal life.[7]

It's never too late to till the ground, pull weeds, and plant for the future. As I've said before, although you can't go back to start a new beginning, you can start now to create a new ending!

INCLINE YOUR EAR TO HEAR FROM GOD

Confused about what to do next? Sweep your mind clear of the debris of anger, the cobwebs of stubbornness, and the clutter of blame shifting. Refuse to cloud your judgment with justification and rationalization. Whether it is your fault or not, take responsibility for securing a solution. Jesus is the ultimate example of this—though He had never sinned or erred, He took the responsibility for all the faults of humanity in order to point the way forward. Accept what He has done for you, and take the initiative to turn things around by turning to God. Pave your path to success by getting the answers you need to produce the fruit you want to grow.

> *Learning to sow to the Spirit is the first step in planting seeds of solution and success in your life.*

We have already talked about insight, foresight, and oversight; let's now talk about hindsight. Think about each stage of your life. From each painful situation that comes to mind, identify the lesson you can learn from it. Use those priceless gems of experience to put your current difficulties into perspective—then ask God to give you His perspective on each situation. What you can see is so very limited. Open your heart and humble yourself before God. Listen for His voice, follow His direction, and He will lift you up.[8]

Seek the Lord while He may be found;
Call upon Him while He is near.
Let the wicked forsake his way
And the unrighteous man his thoughts;
And let him return to the Lord,
And He will have mercy on him,
And to our God,
For He will abundantly pardon.
"For My thoughts are not your thoughts,
Nor are your ways My ways," says the Lord.[9]

Call upon God. Humble yourself before the Lord and allow Him to show you the way—He will light a path for you out of the darkness and make a way for you through the wilderness. But you must take the initiative to ask for the wisdom you need, knowing He will generously give it, for He has given you His Holy Spirit to lead you into all truth.[10] There is no good thing He will withhold from you if you will but ask Him.[11]

> *Challenges do not come to destroy you or cause you duress, but to reveal the strength of your character.*

Remember, difficulties and challenges do not come to destroy you or cause you duress, but to reveal the strength of your character, the relevance of your life, the uniqueness of your identity, the importance of your giftedness, and as a call to discharge your duties and assignments. Immeasurable is the gain from a challenge overcome, priceless is the gift of a triumph in spite of setbacks, and sweeter is a victory won when the chips are stacked against you. Do not shy away from the heat of battle or the challenge to create solutions. It is the very essence of your promotion and prosperity![12]

Plant a thought and reap a word;
plant a word and reap an action;
plant an action and reap a habit;
plant a habit and reap a character;
plant a character and reap a destiny.
—BISHOP BECKWAITH

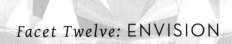

Facet Twelve: ENVISION

SEE WITH NEW EYES

When we are no longer able to change a situation…
we are challenged to change ourselves.[1]
—VICTOR FRANKL

When you begin to see things from Heaven's perspective, the difficulties will feel less overwhelming and the way through will become more evident. As I have said before, we live forward but learn backward. When you retrospectively assess your life, the gems of wisdom you have gained from those precious jewels of experience will continually broaden your perspective—and very often delightfully surprise you.

I have learned that just as no individual encounters an obstacle they don't inherently possess the power to surmount, no nation can be threatened with an economic, social, or political problem that it does not have the collective wisdom to solve. Every trouble can be overcome if properly confronted. Most situations, although stubborn, are not impossible.

> *Persist long enough, believe hard enough, and over time the "impossible" will become possible.*

We simply need to seek divine guidance in solving, eliminating, or capitalizing on them.

99

Think of the dismantling of the Berlin Wall, which most people thought would always divide East and West Germany. The ending of apartheid, the freeing of former colonies, or the thousands of ways God showed George Washington Carver how to profit from the peanut—things that seemed impossible at the time. What about the invention of the airplane? Those afraid of flying were heard to say, "If God wanted man to fly, He would have given him wings!" Flying impossible? Not to the Wright brothers—and certainly not to God.[2] Sixty-six years later, men were walking on the moon!

Persist long enough and believe hard enough, and over time the "impossible" will become possible. Think of Winston Churchill, the man who stood up against the British Parliament when they were certain that winning the war against the Nazis was impossible. "Never, never, never give up" is the wisdom we garner from his biography. When Great Britain refused to surrender, the fate of the world was reversed, and, by the same token, in never giving up so can you reverse your fate. Your perception of what is possible *is* what is possible. Henry Ford said, "Whether you think you can or whether you think you can't, you're right!"

THINK FOR A CHANGE

Nothing is as constant as change. It is perhaps the most natural thing in the world, but it is also the cause of great difficulties. Everybody talks about change, but very few welcome it when it comes. The moment you decide to change, it is often as if everything and everyone suddenly exerts a gravitational pull to keep you the way you are or were. When you change, it will temporarily inconvenience certain people, even though in the long run those same people will benefit from you having increased your capacity to do more on their behalf. By being better and shining brighter you will cause the water table of possibility to rise for everyone.

Also keep in mind, on the other hand, that if you cannot change when circumstances demand it, then you cannot expect others to change. When you're no longer able to deal with a situation, or the situation stubbornly remains after many attempts to change it, the onus is on you to make a personal change. It is you who must exemplify or embody that change, to model and personify the change you're seeking. You can start to think, speak, and act "as if"—you can physically "be" different by how you carry and conduct yourself, from the clothes you wear to your posture. And when you change, everything around you must adjust to accommodate that change.

Og Mandino, one of my favorite inspirational and motivational speakers and an acclaimed best-selling author, was not always viewed as successful. Before he became well known, he was an alcoholic. It is reported that one day, after a long night of drinking, depression drove him to consider suicide. He even stumbled into a pawnshop and purchased a gun. Holding the gun in his hand was one thing, but he couldn't bring himself to pull the trigger. He wandered aimlessly before finding himself in a library. There he decided to transform

You being better and shining brighter will cause the water table of possibility to rise for everyone.

himself by transforming his mind, and a dramatic change began. By consciously and intentionally delivering himself from his own place of despair, simply by changing his mind, he went on to help many others transform their lives.

Could things be the way they are for you because you are the way you are? What one thing can you change about yourself that will change everything?

You can change your mind.

You can change your mind about your station in life, your status in life, or your condition in life. You can change your mind about being disappointed, being mistreated, or being unloved. At the speed of thought you can move from a state of self-pity to self-worth, from thinking, "Woe is me" to "How wonderful is God!"

You will only be transformed to the degree you are able to renew your mind in Christ Jesus.[3] Part of that renewal is learning to lean on and trust in God, "in all things, with prayer and supplication"—because that is how you keep your mind in perfect peace.[4]

SEE POTENTIAL WHEN OTHERS SEE PERIL

Every doubt, every insecurity, every perplexity, every dismal report, financial hardship, emotional struggle, political upheaval, crime, craving, and condition is a prophetic indicator of hidden potential that evil is trying to vanquish. Though meant for destruction, God can turn anything for good if we put our past in His hands and let Him help us build a better future.

When you confront your present condition and acknowledge your problems, you can change them from stumbling blocks into opportunities for growth and development. You must recognize that each problem does indeed hold the key to a brighter future, both for yourself and for humanity as a whole. In every solution that you discover for yourself, you will find the keys to an answer for someone else.

> When we heal the soul of a single person by enabling them to become problem solvers, we give them the tools to transform society.

It is a great day, though tough it may be, when bewildering perplexities take possession of an individual's mind and that person responds with confidence and courage. It signifies that an era of emotional indifference, reckless abandon, immaturity, inexperience, or intellectual numbness has come to an end. It is the mile marker in a person's life when activities grown out of immaturity and self-centeredness lose their satisfaction, and when that person realizes their interconnectedness to all humanity. It is the first step on the road to becoming an aspiring, passionate, purpose-driven, and self-disciplined individual who owns up to his or her part in solving the problems at hand. As a contributing member of a self-healing society, that person will emerge as an inspiration for others challenged by similar conditions. Personal change, no matter how little, makes a big difference in the world—in fact, it makes all the difference. As Mahatma Gandhi was credited with affirming, "We must be the change we want to see in the world."

Those who muster the will to become the change agents God intended—to reflect the nature of the Creator Himself —will be among those who discover the answers to the most perplexing questions facing humanity. When we heal the soul of a single person by enabling them to become problem solvers, we give them the tools to transform society.

Change of this caliber starts from within—at the level of your soul. When you heal your soul, you can heal the world. Your soul, therefore, must be respected, cultivated, and cared for. It houses your consciousness, the home of your moral compass—your inner guide, teacher, advisor, coach—and when calmly listened to and rightly understood, your soul will lead you to a higher degree of understanding and deeper levels of wisdom. Your soul will be a limitless source of inner abundance, ability, and acumen.

Have you ever heard of that old TV dance program, *Soul Train?* Well, think instead of "soul training"—don't run from your problems, but like David did in facing Goliath, run to them! When you do this, you will run straight through them to emerge as a person of greater power and stronger principle, all to the glory of God.

The next time you stand in front of a mirror, take a few moments to face off with your divine self. What you see will surprise you. You will behold the person you have been looking for all of your life—the one who holds the key to solving all of your problems. Resist looking only on the surface. Look within, for the answers lie hidden in the depths of your soul. Look beyond the fear, unbelief, and doubt and see the solution. It is always there, if you will take the time to search for it.

When you change the way you look at things,
the things you look at change.[5]
—DR. WAYNE DYER

PART THREE:

CARAT

The Prospering Power of Purpose

*It is easier to live through someone
else than to complete yourself.
The freedom to lead and plan your own life is frightening
if you have never faced it before.
It is frightening when a [person] finally realizes
that there is no answer to the question "who am I"
except the voice inside.[1]*
—Betty Friedan

Make your work to be in keeping with your purpose.
—Leonardo da Vinci

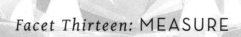

DETERMINE YOUR WORTH

*The measure of a man is the way he
bears up under misfortune.*
—PLUTARCH

Y ou are one of a kind. You are precious to God, and you are of
infinite worth, honored, and loved.[1] You are born with a purpose, intended to prosper, and designed to prevail.

Purpose is derived from the Old French *propos*, which means "to
put forth, intend, or propose," and later the Anglo-French *purpose*, which means "to design."[2] Why is that significant? Because
it means you and I have something to propose, put forth, or
design—and that's not only the prospering power of our purpose,
but also the secret to prevailing. It is your value-added proposition when things get tough. How you bear up under pressure
determines the measure of your worth. When you can harness the
power of your purpose to prevail, you will discover your strength
in hard times.

Your purpose is formed under pressure, just as a diamond is
formed. It's what gives you weight or substance. A unit of weight in
relation to a diamond is called a carat—not to be confused with
"karat," a unit of purity in relation to gold. Both can be used as

a metaphor to shine light on how purpose can provide—or be translated as—a unit of measure. In other words, you have been uniquely endowed with a distinctive purpose; it is the substance of your being, the reason you exist. It's what gives force to your strength and volume to your voice. It's what makes you potent. Likewise, because it is unique to you, its value is only revealed when your authentic brilliance is made to shine.

As we discussed in Part One, a diamond's clarity or purity is also a factor in determining its value. So in this section, we'll take a deeper look at our core beliefs and motivators, and we'll talk more about clarifying your vision and values, leveraging your innate gifts and abilities, and learning to live more authentically. As the refining of gold increases its number of karats, so will refining your aims and goals.

Once you are able to embrace the prospering power of *perspective*, you are poised to exploit the prospering power of *purpose*. Yes, that's a bit of a tongue twister. But here's an even better one: Although purity of purpose will empower you to prevail, it is in the prevailing that your purpose will be purified. The same principles that position you to push through adversities are refined and made stronger in the process. In the next chapter, for example, we will talk about the importance of knowing your "why"—this is a primary driver in moving you forward. The power of your "why" determines how far and how fast you move ahead, up and over, and through whatever barriers you encounter. At the same time, the more barriers you encounter, the more powerful your "why" becomes.

> *How you bear up under pressure determines the measure of your worth.*

We will also look at how strength of purpose enables you to push past rejection, emboldens your resolve, and expands your authority. It will stabilize you in the face of opposition, while at the same time helping you be stabilized by that opposition. As the early nineteenth-century novelist Mary Wollstonecraft Shelley observed, "Nothing contributes so much to tranquilize the mind as steady purpose—a point on which the soul may fix its intellectual eye."[3] Having struggled with hardship and poverty most of her life, Mary Shelley suffered the loss of three of her four children, her husband, health, and reputation, yet she wrote prolifically. She authored one of the most widely read and enduring novels, *The Modern Prometheus*, better known as *Frankenstein*.

We know from history that in the worst of times the courage, resilience, strength, and brilliance of humanity emerges. It is from the crucible of suffering that we see the birth of artistic and literary masterpieces, epic symphonies, and breakthroughs in science, social reforms, and political revolutions. How will you add value to the world around you in times of crisis? What will you offer to design or put forth to help alleviate a need?

> *How will you add value to the world around you in times of crisis?*

Without the pull of a crisis, the urgent demand of a need—the vacuum or void that begs to be filled—we would not be compelled to respond, to take action, or create. But you don't have to wait for some unfortunate situation to improve your current position or the state of the world. You can take creative action now. You can harness the prospering power of purpose.

> *The man without a purpose is like*
> *a ship without a rudder—*
> *a waif, a nothing, a no man.*
> *Have a purpose in life, and having it,*
> *throw such strength in mind and muscle*
> *into your work as God has given you.*
> —THOMAS CARLYLE

"I know the plans I have for you," declares the LORD, "plans to prosper you and not to harm you, plans to give you hope and a future."

Jer. 29:11

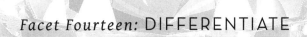

KNOW YOUR WHY

He who has a why to live for can bear almost any how.
—FRIEDRICH NIETZSCHE

Everything that exists in the universe was created to fulfill a purpose.[1] Purpose is the "why" for you being alive. It's what sets you apart and positions you for success. Once you find your why, then the what, the how, and the when take care of themselves. Once you discover your purpose you will be empowered to act decisively, accomplish your goals, make wise choices, and clearly discern what to say "no" to and what you will say a resounding "yes" to. It is in discovering your purpose that you'll be able to do whatever you do with more energy and endurance simply by harnessing the force of your conviction. Knowing your why will provide a springboard that propels you forward and the momentum you need to keep going.

Your purpose will surface in both times of affliction as well as times of affluence. When you are feeling stagnant and powerless, you'll find it is your deeper purpose that empowers you to move forward. By the same token, when you're tempted in a position of power to compromise your values, your greater purpose will be forced to the surface. It will require you to draw that line in the sand and take a stand for what you'll find is your higher calling. It will cause you to differentiate and distinguish yourself as a difference maker.

Your position or station in life does not determine the degree of power you're able to wield. More often than not, as we have seen throughout this book, it is from the underside of adversity—when you are upside down, hung out to dry, or at the bottom of the barrel—that your truth emerges. Like the phoenix rising, you find your spark in the ashes.

This is not only what we've seen throughout history, but also throughout *His*-story as depicted in the Bible. From the Old Testament fathers of faith who rose from the ashes of defeat and despair to become the heroes of their time, to the Lord Himself who endured the Cross in fulfilling His purpose to save the world. They were the privileged, then the scorned, and then the triumphant agents of change—from Moses, to Joseph, to David, to Paul. They had to be denied the power of their position in order to discover the power of their purpose.

> *Knowing your why will provide a springboard that propels you forward and the momentum you need to keep going.*

Interestingly, although we all face challenges, there are none as great as those we face while in privileged positions of power and influence. Let's take a look at a modern-day example of how this can derail us, while at the same time getting us back on track.

THE WINDING ROAD TO WHY

If President Richard Nixon wanted something done, no matter how difficult or how "shady" it was, he would turn to Charles Colson, his "Hatchet Man." When Colson helped Nixon regain the White House in the 1972 presidential election, Colson was at the height of his career, but the experience left him strangely unsatisfied and spiritually parched. As he began to look for answers, even as he wandered the halls of the White House—the very symbol of American power and success—Chuck Colson experienced something unexpected. Meaning and fulfillment were not found in following and promoting a man to the presidency of the most powerful nation on earth; rather, it would later be found in humbling himself to follow the lowly and loving ways of Jesus Christ.

Charles Colson's encounter with Jesus was no meager quoting of a sinner's prayer and committing to show up for church every Sunday. He didn't just schedule God in with the other activities he already had on his calendar. When he met Christ, everything in his life changed. Colson not only asked Jesus for forgiveness for the things he had done, but he also publicly pleaded guilty to them in a court of law, admitting to obstruction of justice. He took responsibility for his actions and was willing to pay the consequences. He didn't fight the charges against him and he was sentenced to serve three years in a federal penitentiary.

Because of his demeanor, however, Chuck Colson served only seven months and was released on good behavior. He was a completely changed man. While most would have put prison behind them and moved on, Chuck sensed the needs of men and women behind bars and saw a vocation in serving them. He started Prison Fellowship and served its cause for the rest of his life—the next thirty-eight years—seeing it expand into 113 nations. He pledged all of the proceeds from his twenty-three books to financing it. Later in life, he founded The Chuck Colson Center for Christian Worldview to help Christians understand the basic tenets of their faith and how to live them out in their communities, just as he had done.

Colson was awarded the Presidential Citizens Medal in 2008 for what the White House website called "his good heart and his compassionate efforts to renew a spirit of purpose in the lives of countless individuals." David Frum, who was a special assistant to President George W. Bush and later became a CNN contributor, tweeted that Colson made his "greatest impact when furthest from power." Lamar Vest, president and CEO of the American Bible Society, called Colson "a powerful example of God's ability to transform a life."[2]

For Chuck Colson, being a new creature in Christ redefined everything. It turned everything he had previously held as true upside down. He went from the halls of power in the White House, serving the most powerful man in the world, to serving the rejected and incarcerated. It was not a logical career choice for someone who wanted to impact the world, yet he did more by serving the lowly than he did in exercising the power of the mighty. His book *Born Again* tells the honest and

> *Be among those who with "great devotion are spent in a worthy cause" and enter the arena willing to face any challenge or opposition head-on.*

forthright story of what changed his life and, consequently, the lives of many others.[3] Mr. Colson passed away in 2012 at the age of 80. The legacy he leaves is one that will continue to touch lives far into the future.

Chuck Colson was a man who faced his problems head-on. Confronted with a Savior who demanded all, he submitted himself to the justice system so that he could face Jesus without having dodged the consequences of his actions. Stripped of his right to serve as an attorney in the great halls of politics, he served as an advocate for the incarcerated instead. Going to prison would have been the end for many men, but for Charles Colson it was the way he found his true life. He faced his problems, and ultimately changed the world for thousands of men and women, and their families, because of it.

I am also reminded of the life of David Wilkerson. He said, "As I look back over fifty years...I recall innumerable tests, trials, and times of crushing pain. But through it all, the Lord has proven faithful, loving, and totally true to all His promises." It is a powerful thought that resonates with the timeless words of Theodore Roosevelt:

It is not the critic who counts; it is not the man who points out how the strong man stumbles, or where the doer of deeds could have done them better. The credit belongs to the man who is actually in the arena, whose face is marred by dust and sweat and blood, who strives valiantly; who errs and comes short again and again; because there is not effort without error and shortcomings; but who does actually strive to do the deed; who knows the great enthusiasm, the great devotion, who spends himself in a worthy cause, who at the best knows in the end the triumph of high achievement and who at the worst, if he fails, at least he fails while daring greatly. So that his place shall never be with those cold and timid souls who know neither victory nor defeat.[4]

This wisdom is not only for individuals. The same holds true for an organization, a family, a government, or a business. Be among those who with "great devotion are spent in a worthy cause" and enter the arena willing to face any challenge or opposition head-on.

Know your "why," and with the courage that comes with great conviction, take your stand. The key to resisting fear is your willingness to differentiate yourself. Your victory will ultimately be determined by your strength of purpose.

Coal that bears up under pressure meets a diamond.
—UNKNOWN

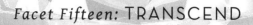

Facet Fifteen: TRANSCEND

PUSH PAST REJECTION

Praise, like gold and diamonds,
owes its value only to its scarcity.
—Samuel Johnson

I take rejection as someone blowing a bugle in my ear
to wake me up and get going.
—Sylvester Stallone

One of the most devastating sources of emotional pain a person can experience is rejection. Rejection has many different faces. And although it is rarely perceived as a blessing, I believe it is often a divine announcement that you were never supposed to prosper within a particular relationship or realm in the first place. Some of us were born into homes, communities, and even nations that reject us. Conversely, some of us place ourselves in relationships or communities that do not have the capacity to prosper us. We turn to individuals or institutions for affirmation. Sometimes, having outgrown an environment or relationship, we still choose to stay in spite of the discomfort and pain. I don't know why we torture ourselves like this, but we too often do. Perhaps we are so afraid of the unknown that we remain with the familiar no matter how repressive it is.

I want to encourage you to try a different approach. When you are confronted with rejection, think of it as a divine course corrector. For example, when it's time for you to move on and you don't, embrace rejection as the push you need to get going. Or when you deviate from a course you have been divinely guided to pursue, understand that rejection might be what keeps you pointed in the right direction. Someone once asked me, "How do you deal with rejection?" My answer? "With grateful acceptance."

Learn how to navigate and use rejection as a tool for growth. It requires a bit of finesse to know when to ignore rejection—when to keep doing what you're doing regardless of what others say—and when to adjust by either changing what you do, or where, or with whom. The key is found in your strength of purpose that is rooted in your identity—knowing who you are in Christ and who God called you to be.

PLAY YOUR HAND WELL

Life can seem like a game of cards. We are dealt a hand by fate, but our destiny is determined by how we play it. A good card player knows when to take risks and how to keep a poker face while doing it. It doesn't matter what the other card players think, it doesn't matter what they talk about or say under their breath. You are focused on simply playing the best game possible with the cards in your hand. That said, you wouldn't let your emotions or strategy be determined by someone else's opinion, because, after all, they can't even see the cards you are holding. The key is to pay attention instead to the cards they are showing and what moves they are making so you can better understand how to play the cards you have in response. Keep your head in the game by focusing on the cards being played, not on who is playing them.

When you are confronted with rejection, think of it as a divine course corrector.

Of course, that's an oversimplistic analogy. Life, as we all know, is built around the dynamics of our relationships. It's our sharing and connection with others that make life meaningful and beautiful. But within the intricacies of those dynamics, you must learn to protect your personal power. Get acquainted with what God has said about you. Know what God has put into you and what His plan is for your life. Keep your dreams alive. No matter where you find yourself now, always be preparing for the next move that will take you closer to the life you envision. Don't waste your time fretting over things said in passing, especially by people who hardly know you. Most won't even remember or think about what they said ever again—so neither should you.

> *You may not be able to change the cards you are dealt, but you can learn to play the hand you have and play it well.*

At the same time, don't run away from constructive criticism or refuse to take personal responsibility to improve the quality of your life. What others say in love can have incredible benefits for helping you grow. With all the handicaps of heredity, the social and psychological complexities that result from how we were raised, not to mention the cultural limitations and economic obstacles we must continually navigate, it is unlikely any of our lives are perfect. You may not be able to change the cards you are dealt, but you can learn to play the hand you have and play it well.

Life, in general, is risky—and the more risks you are willing to take, the more you will risk being rejected. The late, great author William Arthur Ward wrote the following poem entitled, "To Risk":

To laugh is to risk appearing a fool,
To weep is to risk appearing sentimental.
To reach out to another is to risk involvement,
To expose feelings is to risk exposing your true self.
To place your ideas and dreams before

a crowd is to risk their loss.
To love is to risk not being loved in return,
To live is to risk dying,
To hope is to risk despair,
To try is to risk failure.
But risks must be taken because the greatest
hazard in life is to risk nothing.
The person who risks nothing,
does nothing, has nothing, is nothing.
He may avoid suffering and sorrow,
But he cannot learn, feel, change, grow or live.
Chained by his servitude he is a slave
who has forfeited all freedom.
Only a person who risks is free.[1]

Based on the true rags-to-riches story of Chris Gardner, the blockbuster movie *The Pursuit of Happyness* starring Will Smith, highlights what it takes to make it in life. In and out of foster care as a child, this entrepreneur—whose net worth was estimated at $65 million in 2006—was rejected by his wife and then his employer before he wound up homeless on the streets of San Francisco with a young son in the early 1980s. Determined to make it as a stockbroker, he took a position without pay as a trainee at Dean Witter Reynolds. With very little money, Gardner and his son slept in hostels, parks, and public restrooms each night after Gardner had worked as many hours as he could learning how to become a top broker at his firm. It all finally paid off in 1987 when Gardner started his own successful brokerage firm in Chicago.

People usually reject what they don't understand, do not have the capacity for, or cannot control.

Perhaps the rejection you've experienced was the divine push you needed to move on to bigger and better things. Another motivational legend, Tom Hopkins, says, "You are your greatest asset.

Put your time, effort, and money into training, grooming, and encouraging your greatest asset." Always remember, putting your best foot forward will not exempt you from rejection. People usually reject what they don't understand, do not have the capacity for, or cannot control.

Before he died at the age of 47 of pancreatic cancer in July 2008, Randy Pausch offered the following advice: "The key question to keep asking is, 'Are you spending your time on the right things?' Because time is all you have.... And you may find one day that you have less than you think."[2]

ONLY BELIEVE

In a letter defending Bertrand Russell's appointment to a teaching position, Albert Einstein wrote:

> Great spirits have always encountered violent opposition from mediocre minds. The mediocre mind is incapable of understanding the man who refuses to bow blindly to conventional prejudices and chooses instead to express his opinions courageously and honestly.[3]

This is where you must learn to transcend conventional wisdom. Don't "dumb yourself down," "kiss up," or "people please" to avoid rejection. Refuse to blend in at the cost of your individuality. Refuse to be something you're not in order to be accepted. Continue to believe in yourself. Continue to believe in your abilities and in your dreams. You must continue to believe— even when others tell you it can't be done—that it can be done, that your ideals are not too lofty. You must resist the temptation to give up because others do not believe in who you are or in your capabilities.

To overcome rejection, you must believe in yourself. No one ever does anything worthwhile without meeting some kind of opposition in the process. Because of this, it is important to listen to the whispers of God and not the sarcasm or skepticism murmured by others. Believe what God is able to do in and through you. There will always be people who say that your ideas won't work, or that you're not good enough, or that no one would be interested in buying your products or employing your services.

Wayne Gretzky once said, "When I broke into professional hockey at 17, I was told I was too small, too slow and I wouldn't make the NHL."[4] But just look at what he did—he became what many believe to be the greatest individual to ever play professional hockey. Likewise,

> *Your decisions to be, to have, and to do things out of the ordinary demand that you face difficulties that are out of the ordinary.*

George Lucas spent four years shipping the script for *Star Wars* around to the various studios and racking up numerous rejections in the process. If he'd let his negative inner voice get to him he would never have ended up having the highest grossing film of all time.[5]

Look at these other examples of history-makers who were told it couldn't be done:

Albert Einstein was considered an "unteachable" fool by his early teachers.

Michael Jordan was cut from his high school basketball team.

Ludwig Beethoven's music teacher told him he was a hopeless composer.

Colonel Harland Sanders (creator of Kentucky Fried Chicken) was told "no" by over a thousand restaurants for more than a year while he lived in his car trying to sell his chicken recipe.

When **Thomas Edison** was 4, he was sent home from school with a note. The note told his mother that she was to remove her son from school because he was "too stupid to learn."

Walt Disney was turned down by over a hundred banks when he tried to get funding to develop Disneyland. He was also fired from his job at a newspaper for "lacking ideas."

Fred Astaire kept a memo over his fireplace from an MGM testing director after his first screen test that said, "Can't act. Slightly bald. Can dance a little."

Vince Lombardi was told by an expert that he "possesses minimal football knowledge. Lacks motivation."

Enrico Caruso was a famous opera singer who was told by his teacher that he couldn't sing.

Richard Bach, the author of *Jonathan Livingston Seagull*, was turned down by eighteen publishers before finally, in 1970, MacMillan published it. By 1975, this book had sold more than 7 million copies in the U.S.

Mark Victor Hansen and **Jack Canfield** authored the *Chicken Soup for the Soul* series. Fifty book publishers turned them down before somebody finally agreed to take a chance on them. They have since sold over 75 million copies.

George Orwell is most well known for his two books *Animal Farm* and *1984*. *Animal Farm* was rejected by a number of publishers, including one who told him that it was "impossible to sell animal stories in the U.S.A." By 1996, *Animal Farm* had sold 20 million copies and had been translated into 60 languages.[6]

Live your life out loud. Never be bullied into silence or pressured into being a nonentity. Never allow yourself to be made a victim of someone else's insecurities. Accept no one else's proclamations or predictions of doom and failure. Never relinquish your God-given right to define or redefine yourself according to your understanding of who God created you to be.

Your decisions to be, to have, and to do things out of the ordinary demand that you face difficulties that are out of the ordinary. Be bold, and be strong. Be audacious. As John F. Kennedy said, "Let us resolve to be the masters, not the victims, of our history, controlling our own destiny without giving way to blind suspicions and emotions."[7]

To the question of your life, you are the only answer.
To the problems of your life, you are the only solution.[8]
—Jo COUDERT

Facet Sixteen: FORTIFY

GAIN STRENGTH THROUGH COURAGE

We gain strength, and courage, and
confidence by each experience
in which we really stop to look fear in the face.
—ELEANOR ROOSEVELT

If you are to do something great, it takes courage—courage to stand strong in spite of failure, opposition, and ridicule. It takes courage to stand up for what is right, to stand against all odds and to resist the temptation to compromise your morals and convictions in exchange for popularity or influence. It takes courage to move beyond the familiar—what is guaranteed and what gives you a sense of security—in order to pursue your higher calling, to realize a dream or to accomplish a goal. Courage is counter-intuitive because it means that you have to swim against the current or go out on a limb when playing it safe seems the most responsible way to go. It takes courage to leave the shores of certainty to become the Christopher Columbus of your life in order to sail toward destiny's ever-shifting horizons. It takes courage to chart a new course when others insist that embracing the status quo is the most certain way to succeed.

When I think of this kind of courage, I think of Mahatma Gandhi, Nelson Mandela, and Martin Luther King Jr. I also think of Moses, King David, and Queen Esther. More personally, I think of my first mentor—my mother—and also my first coach and my sister, Marilyn, who, in spite of the poverty that plagued our lives, earned two university degrees. She would be the first in my family to attend college and set the standard for the rest of us to follow. Courage comes in all shapes and sizes: Rosa Parks, who refused to sit in the back of the bus, the young man who single-handedly stood down army tanks in Tiananmen Square, my mother who raised seven children on her own, the refugee who crosses the border of a neighboring country in pursuit of a better life, or the teenage girl who chooses not to terminate her pregnancy in spite of restricted resources or support.

The courage that overcomes all fear is the courage that is born of God. It is He who places the divine courage-gene within you, the essence of the power to overcome. He has not given you the spirit of fear, but of power and love and a sound mind.[1] As the Bible states, *"You have already won a victory...because the Spirit who lives in you is greater than the spirit who lives in the world."*[2]

Courage is manifested when you develop a healthy, realistic perspective of who you are in Christ—and when you realize all your Creator has wired you to become and to do. It comes when you say to yourself, "I don't know how I'm going to make it. All I know is that I am." Sadly, many people acquiesce to being the slave of doubt and worry, both of which are grounded in fear-based imagination. Unfounded or baseless fear is a peculiar state of *dis*ease that arises largely out of a lack of knowledge. As the prophet Hosea proclaimed, *"People are destroyed for lack of knowledge."*[3]

> *The courage that overcomes all fear is the courage that is born of God.*

Too many dwindle away and die carrying seeds of greatness, unrealized potential, unwritten books, unsung melodies, undiscovered breakthroughs, and undelivered solutions because of fear. Lack of courage causes divine opportunities and strategic relationships to wither before they ever come to fruition. These opportunities await someone with the strength of courage to do what no one else has done before—who will take on problems that undreamt of innovations and unrealized collaborations will solve.

FACE YOUR FEARS

When you become a slave to unfounded fear, you also become a slave to faulty beliefs, counterproductive behaviors, self-defeating paradigms, ineffective response mechanisms, and shortsightedness, which are all inconsistent with your God-given drive for well-being, success, and prosperity. It is vital that you tap into the courage and power within yourself to reap the benefits associated with their application to every facet of your life.

General Matthew B. Ridgway, who turned the war in Korea to favor the United Nations, once said of courage,

> There are two kinds of courage, physical and moral, and he who would be a true leader must have both. Both are the products of the character-forming process, of the development of self-control, self-discipline, physical endurance, of knowledge of one's job and, therefore, of confidence. These qualities minimize fear and maximize sound judgment under pressure and—with some of that indispensable stuff called luck—often bring success from seemingly hopeless situations.[4]

Courage will cause you to set implausible goals and dare to exceed expectations. Courage is what it takes to accomplish your dreams and realize your vision. It is the incubator of great leaders, innovators, activists, and trailblazers. It causes great achievers and champions to look within themselves to find the mental, moral, emotional, and spiritual strength to pursue their goals, maximize their potential, and to define their destinies. Courage is what it takes to prevail over hardship, pain, disappointment, failure, moral challenges, and mortal danger.

All of us face something that challenges us, some kind of fear—the fear of people, fear of being alone, fear of rejection, fear of failure, fear of change, or fear of commitment. The key is not to avoid your fear or to not feel afraid, but to embrace the fear and proceed anyway.

Many of us have given our personal power away to situations, circumstances, and people. It takes courage to regain it. Courage is the resolve to do something or become something in spite of fear, hardship, obstacles, and opposition. Courage allows you to accept your fear, embrace it as a legitimate emotion, and use it as fuel to accomplish specific goals. Fear is an irrational emotion that accompanies you as you move from the familiarity of your comfort zone into new and unknown territories.

> *Courage is the incubator of great leaders, innovators, activists, and trailblazers.*

Fear is not altogether bad. There are healthy kinds of fear, like the fear of fire or the fear of God. The blessing lies in the effort you make in working toward becoming mentally, emotionally, and spiritually stronger at what you are wired to do until you are empowered to face and conquer whatever fears are holding you back.

Eleanor Roosevelt said, "The danger lies in refusing to face the fear, in not daring to come to grips with it—you must make yourself succeed every time. You must do the thing you think you cannot do." And someone once said to me, "Feel the fear and do it anyway." This is real courage.

"BE STRONG AND OF GOOD COURAGE"

God gave Joshua the encouragement he needed to enter the Promised Land. As a result, Joshua went on to become one of the most powerful commanders in the history of the nation of Israel. He had to learn the art of conditioning his mind to succeed and win by abiding by God's laws of life and leadership. God advised him:

> Be strong and of good courage, for to this people you shall divide as an inheritance the land which I swore to their fathers to give them. Only be strong and very courageous, that you may observe to do according to all the law which Moses My servant commanded you; do not turn from it to the right hand or to the left, that you may prosper wherever you go. This Book of the Law shall not depart from your mouth, but you shall meditate in it day and night, that you may observe to do according to all that is written in it. For then you will make your way prosperous, and then you will have good success.[5]

You must learn the art of mental conditioning. You must exercise your mind by continually aligning it with God's Word of truth. Peter urges you to fortify your mind, to *"gird up the loins of your mind."*[6] In other words, don't quit by giving into your fears. Assume the position of a disciplined warrior and embrace the conqueror you are in Christ![7]

Be strong and courageous and you will overcome and succeed. God has promised it!

How many times did God say, "Be not afraid," throughout the Old and New Testaments? If you hope to change your circumstances, you need courage in order to do so. If you plan to walk away from an abusive relationship, you'll need courage. If you are going to start a new business, you will need courage. To stand up for yourself and face your giants requires courage. In fact, it will take courage to:

- Start over after you have failed.
- Create a new life for you and your family.
- Move from the familiar into the unfamiliar.

- Ask for a raise.

- Resist peer pressure.

- Walk away from opportunities that offer great rewards but compromise your convictions.

- Obey God at the expense of your job, reputation, or position in your community.

- Say "no" when a "yes" is demanded of you.

- Say "yes" when called upon to take responsibility.

- Speak up for yourself or someone else.

- Resist the temptation to retreat because of opposition, criticism, or a lack of support.

- Go out on a limb for something you believe in.

- Maintain your integrity when no one else is looking.

- Be yourself.

- Live for God in an anti-God world.

- Maintain your purity.

- Insist on zero defects and excellence when mediocrity is the standard.

- Break away from the status quo.

- Strive to achieve what people say can never be done.

- Act as a catalyst of change within your organization, government, or community.

- Bridge the gap.

- Set new and clear boundaries.

- Confront your abuser and say, "No more!"

- Say, "I'm sorry," "I made a mistake," "I'm guilty," "You're right and I'm wrong," or "Forgive me."

- Go back to school.

- Start a business.

- Prove your critics wrong.

- Move on.

- Change.

- Dance.

- Write.

- Love again.

- Trust again.

- Believe again.

- Hope again.

Whatever God has placed in your spirit to do or to become, take courage and do it—become it! Go ahead, face your fear and proceed in spite of opposition, for you are well able.[8] Be strong and courageous and you will overcome and succeed. God has promised it, and I not only believe in His promises, I believe in you!

The difference between a successful person and a failure is not that one has better abilities or ideas, superior education or knowledge, the right pedigree, or even an abundance of resources. The difference is that one has the courage to act on his or her ideas and to take calculated risks in spite of the presence of fear, intimidation, or trepidation—and the other does not. Which will you choose to be?

We are told in the Latin proverb: *"Audentes fortuna juvat; fortuna audaces juvat"*—"Fortune favors the bold; fortune favors the brave." And as the Bible urges, *"Continue to be bold for Christ."*[9] *"Be bold and diligent. And God be with you as you do your best."*[10]

Have I not commanded you?
Be strong and of good courage;
do not be afraid, nor be dismayed,
for the Lord your God is with you wherever you go.[11]
—God

Success is never final and failure never fatal.
It is courage that counts.
—Winston Churchill

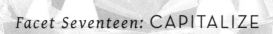

LEVERAGE YOUR UNIQUE ASSETS

Let each man pass his days in that
endeavor wherein his gift is greatest.
—Propertius

Most people stagnate as a result of complacency— something as simple as taking for granted the abilities they already possess, rather than doing more to capitalize on them. Leveraging your unique assets for maximum results requires self-mastery— and that requires discipline, faith, focus, and lots of hard work. Harry Truman said, "In reading the lives of great men, I found that the first victory they won was over themselves. Self-discipline with all of them came first." Of all the talents, skills, trades, and challenges we must learn to master, the most valuable is to master one's self. Motivational icon Jim Rohn believes that we are required to work harder on our own selves than on anything else in life.

Self-mastery will exponentially expand your capacity for success. No matter how difficult your circumstances are, how complicated your life is, or how cruelly you've been treated, you can learn to capitalize on whatever little you currently have by mastering your thoughts, words, habits, time, and yes, skills. You are the captain of your soul and the master of your fate[1]—nobody but you can make the most of what you already have. And with God's help all things are possible.

The great socio-psychologist Abraham Maslow developed what he called the "Hierarchy of Human Needs," which is a pyramid representing the five levels of human development, with the need for survival at the very base. Each progressive level of human experience advances up the pyramid until self-actualization is depicted at the apex. An individual reaches this ideal state of being once they have "self-actualized"—the key word here being *self*. A person is not "actualized" by society, culture, governments, or institutions, but only by one's own internal nature or sense of individuality. One of the determinants of having "self-actualized," according to Maslow, is the ability to see problems as scenarios that require solutions rather than reasons for complaining or making excuses. Therefore, before you can become the master of your surroundings, you must first learn to master yourself.

> *Before we can become masters of our surroundings, we must become masters of ourselves.*

In *Prelude to Chaos*, author John Patrick defines self-actualization as "the desire to become more and more of what one is—to become everything that one is capable of becoming."[2] According to author Kurt Goldstein, self-actualization is "the tendency to actualize as much as possible [one's] individual capacities."[3] The tendency toward self-actualization is "the only drive by which the life of the organism is determined."[4] In other words, the innate desire to self-actualize is a driving force that will ultimately lead to the maximizing of one's abilities and the realization of one's destiny, what we might call "self-determination."

We are all called upon to make a declaration of our independence. Interestingly, although the Declaration of Independence is one of the shortest legislative documents in the history of the United States, it is considered to be one of the best written. This is because it holds within it the fundamental human aspirations for which freedom is prized. As Dr. Clenard Childress states:

> The chief cornerstone of truth by which Dr. Martin Luther King and others of the Civil Rights movement staked their claim for social justice is recorded in the Declaration of Independence which says, "We hold these truths to be self-evident, that all Men are created equal, that they are endowed by their Creator with certain unalienable Rights, that among these are Life, Liberty and the Pursuit of Happiness."[5]

Today I challenge you that instead of making a declaration of independence make a declaration of dependence on God. Without His grace we are nothing. Without His assistance we can never truly and totally become all that we have the potential to be.

No matter what a person's socioeconomic status or occupation, he or she can become a virtuoso at whatever they do by learning the art of self-mastery.

Martin Luther King Jr. once said, "I have a dream that my four little children will one day live in a nation where they will not be judged by the color of their skin, but by the content of their character." On December 27, 1962, while in Nashville, Tennessee, Dr. King said something similar, referring to the Declaration of Independence:

> This idea of the dignity and worth of human personality is expressed eloquently and unequivocally in the Declaration of Independence. Never has a sociopolitical document proclaimed more profoundly and eloquently the sacredness of human personality.[6]

He later went on to say:

Even if it falls your lot to be a street sweeper, go on out and sweep streets like Michelangelo painted pictures; sweep streets like Handel and Beethoven composed music; sweep streets like Shakespeare wrote poetry; sweep streets so well that all the host of heaven and earth will have to pause and say, "Here lived a great street sweeper who swept his job well."[7]

In other words, no matter what a person's socioeconomic status or occupation, he or she can become a virtuoso at whatever they do by learning the art of self-mastery.

What Is a Human Being Worth?[8]

Numerous people have invested an enormous amount calculating the composition and worth of the human body. Using basic scientific methods, they totaled the monetary value of the most basic elements in our bodies. The sum total will shock you. According to some studies, and although these studies are limited in scope, the average human being is worth less than $5.00.

For example, the Imperial State Institute for Nutrition at Tokyo developed a method for measuring the value of a person's skin. It was determined that the average person is the proud owner of fourteen to eighteen square feet of skin. Relative to the price of cowhide—sold for approximately $.25 per square foot—the value of an average person's hide is about $3.50 to $4.00.

The U.S. Bureau of Chemistry and Soils invested many a hard-earned tax dollar in calculating the chemical and mineral composition of the human body, which breaks down as:

- 65 percent oxygen,
- 18 percent carbon,
- 10 percent hydrogen,
- 3 percent nitrogen,

- 1.5 percent calcium,
- 1 percent phosphorous,
- 0.35 percent potassium,
- 0.25 percent sulfur,
- 0.15 percent sodium,
- 0.15 percent chlorine,
- 0.05 percent magnesium,
- 0.0004 percent iron,
- 0.00004 percent iodine.

There are also trace quantities of fluorine, silicon, manganese, zinc, copper, aluminum, and arsenic—all too infinitesimal to calculate. The combined elements were valued at less than a dollar.

However, based on stock market fluctuations, these values are subject to change. Since the majority of noted studies leading to this conclusion were conducted by the U.S. and Japan, you will need to consult the New York Stock Exchange, NASDAQ, the Nikkei Index, and perhaps the London Stock Exchange to determine your current worth in the marketplace. Taken alone, however,

> *We cannot move a finger or bat our eyes without electrical charges being involved and without, literally, "making waves."*

these figures give reason to understand why the world devalues human life.

Thank God that your most valuable asset is not your skin or mineral composition, but your brain, which controls and regulates your body. The brain is a magnificent bioelectric and biochemical machine comprised of electrons and atoms of which it can be truly said, "The whole is greater than the sum of its parts." The electrons and atoms within your body are not just cellular constituents or particles of matter, but waves of living energy, and not just any energy, but divine energy—the very essence of God Himself.

I have had the profound opportunity to see a drop of blood placed under a high-powered microscope. To my amazement, at the very center of that drop of blood I witnessed a spark of light. Scripture states, *"God is light."*[9] Each one of us has been made in His image and after His likeness. This is why God calls us *"the light of the world."*[10]

I have read that researchers calculated that if the electronic energy of the hydrogen atoms in the human body could be collected, a single person could supply the electrical needs of a country for nearly a week. One noted theorist[11] claimed that the atoms in our bodies contain a potential energy charge of more than 11 million kilowatt hours per pound. He also estimated that if this is correct, the energy produced by the average person is worth nearly $85 billion. Moreover, while remaining totally undetectable to the human eye, these electrons and atoms are not just particles of matter, but waves of living energy that ripple out in patterns, reflecting and affecting the molecular configuration of the environment in which we live and interact.

The human body is an electro-chemical machine; we cannot move a finger or bat our eyes without electrical charges being involved and without, literally, "making waves." In the early 1950s, Dr. W. Jerome Stowell and a team of nuclear scientists set out to measure the wavelength of electrical charges emitted by the brain as it passed from life to death. A woman who was terminally ill and lay dying, but was otherwise alert and sound of mind, was chosen as their test subject. An electronic charge-measuring device and a tiny microphone were placed nearby. In an adjoining room, the team of scientists watched an instrument that showed a needle pointing to zero at the center, with a scale ranging to 500 points on either side—negatively to the left and positively to the right. An identical device had been used to measure the power emitted by a 50,000-watt broadcasting station. A message sent around the world registered at nine points on the positive scale. Dr. Stowell reported the following as the scientists witnessed the final moments of the dying woman's life:

> As the last moments of the lady's life arrived, she began to pray and praise the Lord. She asked Him to be merciful to those who had despitefully used her. Then she reaffirmed her faith in God, telling Him she knew He was the only power. ...He always had been and always would be. ...She told Him how much she loved Him.
>
> We scientists had been so engrossed with the woman's prayer that we had forgotten our experiment. We looked at each other and saw tears streaming down scientific faces.
>
> Suddenly we heard a clicking sound on our forgotten instrument. We looked and the needle was registering a positive 500, desperately trying to go higher only to bounce against the 500 positive post in its attempt!
>
> By actual instrumentation we had recorded that the brain of a woman, alone and dying in communication with God had registered more than 55 times the power used by a 50,000 watt broadcasting station sending a message around the world.[12]

The same team of scientists then sought to measure the wavelength of electric charges emitted by the brain of a patient known for his hostility toward the hospital staff. During one of his angry outbursts when he cursed and took the Lord's name in vain, the instrument showed the needle registering in the negative direction at the far left. Dr. Stowell offered the following conclusion:

> By actual instrumentation we had registered what happened in the brain, when that brain broke one of God's Ten Commandments, "Thou shalt not take the name of the Lord thy God in vain."

We had established by instrumentation the positive power of God and the negative power of the adversary. We had found that beneficial truth is positive, and non-beneficial things covered by the "Thou shall nots" of the Ten Commandments are negative.

If we scientists can record these things, I believe with all my heart that the Lord God can keep a record of our thoughts.[13]

Since discovering the findings of those experiments, the formerly atheistic doctor dedicated his life to serving God. Dr. Stowell became a vocal activist for the cause of Christ, proclaiming, "It is the presence of God in us that gives us power, of whose magnitude we have no conception."

Every day of your life you are transmitting an energy that creates an atmosphere around you. Some call it an aura, others think of it as an attitude or personal presence. Whatever you choose to call it, this force creates a positive or negative magnetic field. Like attracts like. If this energy is faith-filled, you will attract the positive equivalence in physical or experiential manifestations—if it is fear-filled, you will attract the opposite. You must have faith in the God who created you,[14] that you are not a glitch, a mishap, a haphazard compilation of molecules, or a random product of your environment. You are much more powerful than that. You were created with great purpose and power, with the very nature of God and the mind of Christ.[15]

You were created with great purpose and power—with the very nature of God and the mind of Christ.

If we could reproduce the human brain or replicate its functionality, this undertaking would cost untold billions of dollars. Scientists report that we utilize less than 10 percent of the capacity of our brain. In truth, we use closer to 2 percent. So, if you were able to tap in to the remaining 98 percent, imagine what you could do! What would happen if instead of wasting brain energy on worry, doubt, anger, frustration, and fear, you instead focused that energy on creativity, compassion, hope, forgiveness, and joy?

Perhaps if you were to actually see your potential from God's perspective and believe that He made you to reflect His divine genius, you might stop listening to what others say about you and start tapping in to the hidden source of your power—*God Himself.* You would take delight in disciplining yourself and cultivating your potential. You would do everything necessary to rid yourself of self-defeating thoughts and behaviors.

Paul the apostle exclaimed, *"We have this treasure in earthen vessels."*[16] Remember, it is not the vessel that makes the contents valuable, but the contents that make the vessel valuable!

VALUE BEYOND CALCULATION

You are an immensely powerful and valuable being. You are a divine masterpiece—unique and important. You are unlike anyone who has ever lived or ever will live after you are gone. You are one of a kind and the only one qualified to be you. That's something to think about.

Why would you want to devalue yourself by being a poor copy of someone else? God has left a genetic encryption of your unique potential within your DNA. Matt Ridley, in his book *Genome,* breaks a human being, a *genome,* down like this:

Imagine that the genome is a book.

There are twenty-three chapters, called chromosomes.

Each chapter contains several thousand stories, called genes.

Each story is made up of paragraphs, called exons, which are interrupted by advertisements, called introns.

Each paragraph is made up of words, called codons.

Each word is written in letters called bases.

There are one billion words in the book, which makes it…as long as 800 Bibles. If I read the genome out to you at the rate of one word per second for eight hours a day, it would take me a century. If I wrote out the human genome, one letter per millimeter, my text would be as long as the River Danube.[17]

You truly are an extravagant work of art.

Given these facts, when do you have time to do anything else but what you have been wired to do? When do you have time to worry about what others think about you? Or to aimlessly fret over the difficulties life sets in your path? The human genome does not need your help to do what it was created to do. It both replicates and duplicates; the only thing you have to do is cooperate.

Jesus said, *"Behold, I have come—in the volume of the book it is written of Me—to do Your will, O God."*[18] When God speaks through a prophet about you, it is like reading a volume of a book that contains your life's purpose and destiny, that which He has prepared for you since before the foundation of the world. You have been wired for success and

> *How will you face each day—each problem— knowing you are a walking, breathing, and destiny-driven, miracle-inspired masterpiece?*

filled with the breath of divine energy. Peter states that we are *"partakers of the divine nature."*[19] You and I, every single one of us, is a divine masterpiece. How will you face each day—each problem—knowing you are a walking, breathing, destiny-driven, miracle-inspired masterpiece?

It is time to live like the miracle you are. God did not place you on this earth to be beaten down by circumstances or defeated by difficulties. Your existence is not meant to be a comedy of errors; it was intended to be an action-packed adventure! It is time to lift yourself up, dust yourself off, and get on with the business of being who you were created to be.

*If you begin to understand what you are
without trying to change it, then what you
are undergoes a transformation.*[20]
—JIDDU KRISHNAMURTI

*We are what we think.
All that we are arises with our thoughts.
With our thoughts we make the world.
Speak or act with an impure mind
and trouble will follow you as the wheel
follows the ox that draws the cart.*[21]
—THOMAS BYROM

Facet Eighteen: INTEGRATE

LIVE AUTHENTICALLY

Often, it's not about becoming a new person,
but becoming the person you were
meant to be and already are,
but don't know how to be.[1]
—HEATH L. BUCKMASTER

If I asked you the question, "Who are you?" would you answer with the role you play, what you do for a living, or the title you wear? I find it interesting how many people don't know who they truly are at the core of their being. People are always saying, "I'm trying to find myself," "I don't know what I want," or "I don't know where I'm going." Some pursue marriage in the hopes of finding themselves, while others pursue academic degrees, and others have children. But do they really ever find themselves? Do they ever get clear on where they're going or what they want from life?

How can you begin to live authentically if you don't know who you are?

I'll bet people have been telling you who they think you should be all of your life, but let me ask you this question: Who does God say you are? When you look into the mirror of the Word,[2] do you see yourself there? What does it say about who you *really* are and why you're here?

I know one thing for sure: You are not a mistake and you are not the sum total of your past mistakes. Refuse to define yourself by your past. Resist defining yourself by your roles and titles, for you are so much more. You are more than your current status, situation, or circumstances. Get an eternal perspective of your identity and worth—what you're capable of—and why you should pursue it with your whole heart. Familiarize yourself with what God says about you. How you honor who He created you to be is what counts before God. That's the kind of person the Father is searching for—those who are simply and honestly themselves, who fully live in the uniqueness with which they were created.

> *How you honor who He created you to be is what counts before God.*

Ask God to show you who you are in His eyes. Your authentic, divine self is the seed of greatness God put on the inside of you, the deposit God made when He formed *"Christ in you, the hope of glory."*[3] It is who God has lovingly crafted you to be. Steve Maraboli says:

> Live authentically! Why would you compromise something that's beautiful to create something that is fake? …
> You were put on this earth to achieve your greatest self, to live out your purpose, and to do it fearlessly.[4]

We often lose ourselves when we live outside-in rather than inside-out. We make ourselves vulnerable to the push and pull of external forces. Personal growth is a process of living your truth, no matter what is going on around you, and no matter what others say or how they respond to you.

I don't know where you are on your journey of self-discovery, and I don't know how much you have achieved relative to your goals, dreams, and visions. Maybe you are somewhat like me— even though you might have accomplished many wonderful things in life, like earning a degree (or several), securing a successful career, starting a profitable business, building your dream home or purchasing your dream car—there is still a great deal for you to do before you call it quits. Wherever you are on your journey, I promise you if you apply the principles here, you will be better tomorrow than you are today.

Take a moment to reflect on who you are relative to who you know you should be. Do you feel that you are living authentically? What areas do you feel you should work on? Personal growth begins with you. Because it's a process involving change, it will require you to abandon your comfort zone. You must accept that nothing is constant. But most importantly, living authentically requires mindfulness, intention, self-discipline, and a whole lot of courage—courage, I know, that has already been seeded into your heart.

> " *Problems can be the catalysts that take you from wondering who you are to a place of grounded authenticity—rooted in your identity and purpose.* "

THROUGH THE VALLEY TO THE OTHER SIDE

Are you currently living the life of your dreams? Are you living the best, blockbuster version of your life or a mediocre B-movie version of someone else's? How intentional and insightful are you when it comes to the challenges you face?

If addressed correctly, problems can be the catalysts that take you from wondering who you are to a place of grounded authenticity that is rooted in your identity and purpose. Problems force you to look at yourself with new eyes and demand that you find the courage to clear the clutter from your mind, soul, and spirit so you can live with the freedom that comes from clarity. The debris of the past must be purged so that you can press in to your best future. Being decisive by confronting your current problems head-on will help you determine what you really want and what you truly value.

Accept no one's definition of how you should be—nor anyone's narrative of how you should live. The stories you believe about yourself will shape you. "Everyone tells a story about themselves inside their own head. Always. All the time," writes novelist Patrick Rothfuss. "That story makes you what you are. We build ourselves out of that story."[5]

Instead, listen to who God says you are. What's the narrative He is offering you? Embrace the authentic person He has created you to be. Being anything other than who you are is to betray the God-inspired nature that He has entrusted you with.

This type of authenticity requires right thinking. As Paul instructed, always be:

> *Filling your minds and meditating on things true, noble, reputable, authentic, compelling, gracious—the best, not the worst; the beautiful, not the ugly; things to praise, not things to curse. Put into practice what you learned from me, what you heard and saw and realized. Do that, and God, who makes everything work together, will work you into His most excellent harmonies.*[6]

Don't get caught limping between opinions. Be decisive. Know who and whose you are, and allow only that to define you. Take a few moments to look over the following chart that compares the attributes of an authentic life to an inauthentic one:

AUTHENTIC SELF	INAUTHENTIC SELF
Is empowered	Is impotent— gives personal power away
Has a vision for life	Lives from day to day, going wherever the wind blows
Lives inside-out	Lives outside-in
Is proactive	Is reactive

AUTHENTIC SELF	INAUTHENTIC SELF
Lives from their core	Lives by external loci of control
Is confident in who they are	Is insecure
Fosters healthy relationships	Relationships are dysfunctional and unhealthy
Feels at peace	Feels anxious
Feels optimistic	Feels pessimistic
Is open	Is closed
Commits	Is afraid of commitment
Is flexible	Is inflexible and rigid
Cooperates	Criticizes
Lives true to their convictions	A people-pleaser
Practices tolerance and celebrates differences in others	Is intolerant
Is secure about who they are	Is insecure and doubting
Is confident in their decision-making	Lacks confidence in their decision-making
Thinks for self, but listens to others	Relies on others to think and doesn't contribute ideas
Is credible	Lives a life of duplicity
Negotiates win/win solutions	Fights to win at all costs or accepts losing too easily
Wants to do their personal best	Wants to do just enough to get by
Conducts their affairs with integrity	Cannot be trusted
Takes a stand	Goes with the flow
Knows when to apologize	Rationalizes mistakes and/or blames others
Takes personal responsibility, sometimes even when others are at fault	Avoids taking responsibility
Accepts constructive criticism	Is defensive and justifies everything
Listens to feelings	Is disconnected from feelings
Makes healthy choices	Acts on impulse
Knows when to stop and reevaluate	Burns out
Interdependent	Independence keeps them from knowing when to ask for help
Lives a dynamic life with freedom	Lives a life of limitations and addictions

AUTHENTIC SELF	INAUTHENTIC SELF
Thinks before acting and/or speaking	Is impetuous— often later regrets things said or done
Tells the truth	Placates and lies
Cooperates with others	Is in a state of constant conflict
Challenges themselves to be their best	Only cares about impressing others
Shares feelings openly	Hides or denies feelings
Is challenged to grow by adversity	Is victimized and uses addictive behaviors to "cope"
Uses freedom to enhance self and others	Uses freedom to self-destruct
Is motivated by clear intention	Is paralyzed by indecision
Is faith-filled and passionate	Is confused and overwhelmed
Is positive and optimistic	Is negative, depressed, and frustrated
Is creative and innovative	Gets bogged down in endless mind clutter
Respects the rights of others	Disrespects others
Recognizes and respects boundaries	Is enmeshed in unhealthy relational constellations; codependent
Maintains healthy, mutually-beneficial relationships	Relationships are toxic, one-sided, and abusive
Exhibits depth of character	Lacks integrity
Reliable and committed	Wishy-washy and fly-by-night
Lives with vision and clear goals	Lacks vision, and goals are sketchy, at best
Is disciplined and focused	Is undisciplined and easily distracted
Forgives	Is unforgiving
Releases	Holds on
Competes with self and wins	Competes with others
Stands out	Blends in
Overcomes	Underachieves
Thrives in spite of their environment	Is diminished due to their environment

Choose to live authentically. From this point forward, be willing to recognize and resist being inauthentic—a less-than-best version of yourself. Be true to who you are. It is time to get in the game and show everyone what you can really do!

AUTHENTICITY LEADS TO SELF-ACTUALIZATION

You have to fight to live authentically. You are the best-qualified person to be you, to fill your part of the puzzle. You are gifted, skilled, and talented—called and anointed. You have something to contribute, to give, to build, to sing, to create, to engineer; no one else has your part, and no one else can sing it like you can! You are a divine masterpiece—a miracle in motion. Within you are the keys to not only your future success, but also someone else's. You are the answer to someone's prayer. You hold the keys to someone else's victory. And it is for that very reason you will face opposition from the enemy. Simply by virtue of the Christ in you, you will experience opposition.

Your response to life's challenges and adversities will determine the degree to which you self-actualize.

There's no way around it. If you are alive, you will have problems. But praise God and rejoice—it is so much better than the alternative! At the end of the day, it's not what happens to you that defines you; it is how you respond to what happens to you that defines you. Respond from a place of authentic power because your response to life's challenges and adversities will determine the degree to which you self-actualize.

A self-actualized person is someone who leverages his or her potential, a person who is fully engaged in excavating and capitalizing on his or her unique assets, not as a spectator, but as a full participant in the arena of life. They don't make excuses but accept personal responsibility for being the change they want to see in the world. They give of their lives with everything they have to offer, knowing that *"giving, not getting, is the way. Generosity begets generosity,"* that if you *"give away your life; you'll find life given back, but not merely given back—given back with bonus and blessing."*[7]

Are you willing to give away your life for what you believe in, to discipline yourself to accomplish what you are called to do? Will you, with unfailing determination and unfaltering faith, love, and generosity, take the actions necessary to bring it to pass? No one can decide these things for you. Only you can determine your course and remain true to your path, as Shakespeare wrote in *Hamlet*:

> *This above all: to thine ownself be true*
> *And it must follow, as the night the day*
> *Thou canst not then be false to any man.*
> (ACT I, SCENE III)

By the same token, Henry David Thoreau counseled, "If a man does not keep pace with his companions, perhaps it is because he hears a different drummer. Let him step to the music which he hears, however measured or far away."[8] Harvey S. Firestone concurred by advising, "Accept no one's definition of your life, but define yourself."

You are an original—one of a kind. Your worth is beyond measure. All that is required of you is to be true to yourself at all times. Face your fears with courage, refuse to be seduced into feeling victimized, and change your perception of the problems currently challenging you. No matter how things look, all things are working for your good.[9] The best is yet to come.

> *So, friends, confirm God's invitation*
> *to you, His choice of you.*
> *Don't put it off; do it now.*
> *Do this, and you'll have your life on a firm footing.*[10]
> —PETER

Once we believe in ourselves, we can risk
curiosity, wonder, spontaneous delight,
or any experience that reveals the human spirit.
—E. E. CUMMINGS

PART FOUR:

CUT

THE PROSPERING POWER OF PERSEVERANCE

*For a long, long time it had seemed to me
that I was about to begin real life.
But there was always some obstacle in the way,
something to be gotten through first,
some unfinished business, time still to
be served, a debt to be paid.
Then life would begin.
At last it dawned on me that these
obstacles were my life.*
—ALFRED SOUZA

UNCOVER YOUR TRUE BRILLIANCE

Whether we fall by ambition, blood, or lust,
like diamonds we are cut with our own dust.[1]
—JOHN WEBSTER

We have covered a great deal of territory as we've explored how to shine brighter through the hard times we encounter. We've discussed how clarity of vision can help us to not only overcome but to even prosper from the problems we face. We've talked about how perspective colors our world and that by changing the way we look at things, things will change the way they look. We have also learned how our strength of purpose empowers us to add value to the world and therefore expands our effectiveness and worth—how a powerful "why" trumps any obstacles of "how." We talked about the value of authenticity. With every hardship and triumph we become more clear about who we are and what we're made of, refining our vision of who we can be and strengthening our resolve to remain true to who we are.

Living authentically also gives us the power to persevere. In fact, as we talk about the fourth "C" in relation to a diamond's worth, its *cut*, we will be talking more about how your authentic brilliance is revealed. You've heard it said that the more a diamond is cut, the brighter it sparkles. As we have learned, each cut is called a facet. Every trial, failure, hardship, and defeat that you face reveals another facet of your character, another occasion to reflect the light of God's grace. The same is true with every opportunity you have to forgive or to apologize—it makes you shine a little brighter. God lifts up the humble and shows mercy to those who show mercy. He promises that the more you give, the more you'll be given; the more you lose your life, the more life you'll find; and more metaphorically, the more you're cut, the more you'll sparkle. This is the prospering power of perseverance.

This is why James exhorts, "Let patience have her perfect work," for it is the art of being perfected.[2] We are perfected through our persevering, for it's what brings out the best in us—what we might never have thought possible otherwise. How else will we be driven to push the envelope—to not only venture to think outside of the box, but to dare climb out of it? To persevere we will be required to identify and face our greatest personal challenges, to elevate our attitude to increase our aptitude, and be willing to do what needs to be done until we get it right. It is in the persevering that we are polished to perfection.

> *Every trial, failure, hardship, and defeat that you face reveals another facet of your character—another occasion to reflect the light of God's grace.*

I can't think of a better illustration than the real-life story of two tennis greats, Venus and Serena Williams. They beautifully exemplify each of the four principles we have presented. They show us how to approach every problem from a place of empowerment with a future-focused perspective and deep-seated purpose—and then how to persevere until they've beaten the odds, torn down the barriers, and broken world records to become legendary icons in their own lifetimes.

PERSEVERANCE PERSONIFIED

Venus and Serena Williams have dominated the world of professional tennis for more than a decade. Each is a resounding success in her own right, overcoming poverty and racism on the journey from the ghetto to Center Court at Wimbledon.

Venus and Serena were the youngest of five sisters, raised in Compton, California, the hub of Los Angeles County and one of the most crime- and poverty-ridden neighborhoods in the United States. The five girls all shared one bedroom with two bunk beds for a good portion of their childhood. Serena, the youngest, didn't have a bed of her own, so she slept with a different sister each night.

When Serena was three and Venus was four years old, their dad, Richard Williams, watched a tennis match on TV one night and heard the commentator remark on how much money one of the players had earned that week. The amount was more than he made in a year! He realized that tennis could provide the family with an opportunity for a better life. That night he made a decision: to turn his daughters into tennis champions.

But there was one problem. He didn't know how to play tennis. So he and his wife set about mastering the game using how-to books and instructional videos. They took all five of the girls out to the rundown public courts at a nearby park. It soon became apparent that while the three oldest girls didn't have an aptitude for the game, the two youngest, Serena and Venus, showed promise.

At the ages of three and four, the girls began their training on those cracked courts, often having to clear away broken glass and garbage before they could play. It wasn't uncommon to hear the sound of gunfire echoing through the park while they practiced, as drive-by shootings were commonplace in that area. But the girls kept at it and won the respect of those who watched their determination in practice. It wasn't long before a local gang took to hanging around the courts while they played, not to harm them, but to protect them from anyone who might try.

By the time they were nine and ten, their father had managed to raise enough money from sponsors to move the family to Florida. Eventually both girls were dominating the junior circuit before turning professional in their early teens. At the writing of this book, Venus has garnered seven Grand Slam singles titles, four Olympic gold medals (one in singles, three in doubles with Serena), and is recognized as having the fastest-clocked serve in women's tennis ever recorded. Serena has won a total of fifteen Grand Slam singles titles and three Olympic gold medals in doubles with her sister Venus.

You have to believe in yourself when no one else does—that makes you a winner right there.

Together they also have thirteen Grand Slam women's doubles titles and each has won two mixed doubles Grand Slam tournaments.

On the road to success, the Williams sisters had to deal with racism and personal tragedies, including the death of one of their older sisters. However, they are living proof of the power of intention, discipline, focus, positive thinking, hard work, and overcoming faith. Undaunted by their seemingly hopeless situation and the negativity they encountered along the way, they rose to be triumphant and dominate women's tennis.

Both Venus and Serena live by the wisdom of Jesus Christ. Serena's favorite quote is from the movie *Spiderman*: "With great power, comes great responsibility." They are passionate about paying it forward by helping others reach their full potential and realize their dreams. They want others to have the attitudes of winners too. As Venus once put it: "Some people say that I have an attitude—maybe I do. But I think that you have to. You have to believe in yourself when no one else does—that makes you a winner right there."

I couldn't have said it better myself. That is what it is all about: finding your place of power and influence so that you can believe in yourself even when no one else does. And then, to persist in pursuing your dream no matter the opposition you face. That is the path of a world-changer and champion in the game of life.

That is the path we should all be on.

> *Never mind searching for who you are.*
> *Search for the person you aspire to be.*
> —ROBERT BRAULT

IDENTIFY YOUR GREATEST CHALLENGE

*Adversity is the diamond dust Heaven
polishes its jewels with.*
—Thomas Carlyle

We all have been to that place where a broken heart, broken dreams, or broken promises have made us want to throw in the towel. But this is life. And life isn't just arbitrarily happening to you—you are happening to it as well. You might not have chosen how it began, but you can choose how it ends. You have the freedom to choose how you live between the start and finish lines.

For many of us, that is our greatest challenge—simply taking responsibility for the outcomes we desire and the consequences we experience is more than we are willing to do. It's not our weaknesses and wrongdoings that trip us up most, but simply being willing to identify and admit to them.

Revealing your true strength will require you to take a deeper look within yourself, to be willing to cast off the weights and get rid of the baggage, to abandon what is unnecessary, cut away the superficial, and throw away your crutches—whatever isn't serving your higher calling. That kind of self-examination will require you to become vulnerable, and that takes courage. When you courageously step out of your comfort zone and accept the challenge to find new life strategies for overcoming and solving old problems—persist in the midst of unfavorable situations—you give yourself permission to grow, to maximize your potential, and to discover the greatness within.

Some people believe that God orchestrates every problem that enters their life. But this is not true. In His omniscience, He knows about them, and in His sovereignty, He may allow them. However, many problems are a result of our own doing—a result of the inescapable law of cause and effect. Once you are able to embrace this truth, you will be in a position to take control of the state and quality of your life.

Taking responsibility for your thoughts and actions—no matter how tempted you may be to blame your government, the economy, your upbringing, or other people—will empower you to alter the course of your destiny. By focusing on the life you desire to create rather the life you wish to eradicate, you will learn that the power within is greater than the negative forces without.

> *Every experience is a capacity-building opportunity that you can learn and grow from.*

You may not see it now, but as you consider that perhaps some of the outward turmoil you're experiencing may indeed be a reflection of the inner turmoil of your mind and emotions, you will begin to realize how powerful of an individual you really are. Every experience is a capacity-building opportunity that you can learn and grow from. All things—the good and what may seem bad—are working together for your edification and maturity.

Paul reminded the Romans of much this same thing: *"We also glory in our sufferings, because we know that suffering produces perseverance; perseverance, character; and character, hope,"*[1] further adding,

"All things work together for good to those who love God...in all these things we are more than conquerors."[2]

SOW TO THE FUTURE, REAP FROM THE PAST

Most of our perplexing and challenging issues come from what Margaret Wheatley would call "unintended consequences." She said, "Without reflection, we go blindly on our way, creating more unintended consequences, and failing to achieve anything useful."[3]

Many of us live on the edge—teetering between right and wrong, good and evil, morality and immorality, integrity and compromise, sanity and insanity. Desperation, impatience, or impulsiveness threatens to push us over the edge. We don't want to create; we just want to cut corners, take the easy way out, or just plain cheat; we look for shortcuts out of the ditch into which we have fallen or the valley of despair into which we have mistakenly wandered. Too often we

> *We live forward and learn backward. We sow to the future and reap from the past.*

opt to take the road of least resistance in an attempt to mitigate the pain, humiliation, shame, and discomfort associated with the consequences of our past choices.

If you look back at where you have traveled, you will discover that any shortcut you attempted to take defaulted to the proverbial "long road home." In each ill-thought-out scenario and perplexing circumstance, if you had known better, perhaps you would have made different decisions and acted in a different manner. Hindsight is always 20/20; if you had only known better, you would have done better. Perhaps your decisions would have been based on the future you wanted and the world you envisioned living in, rather than myopically addressing an immediate crisis without consideration of the long-term consequences. Eradicating the pain associated with "present realities" is not the same as deliberately constructing a better future.

We live forward and learn backward. We sow to the future and reap from the past. Imagine if we'd only known that every solution we were looking for was already inside of us from the beginning. If we had increased our faith in God and His ability to enlarge our capacity[4]—to grant us wisdom and ingenuity[5]—many of us would have avoided the unfortunate collision with calamity that left our lives, marriages, finances, reputation, and influence shipwrecked.

However, there remains that proverbial pot of gold at the end of the rainbow—the "unintended consequence" that may bring temporary sorrow or hardship, but can yield a long-term blessing if it is carefully examined rather than bemoaned. In other words, if you are willing to confront those consequences and invest creative energy to learn from your mistakes and overcome them, there is no limit to the good that can come out of the solutions you'll find.

THE LAW OF OPPOSITE EFFECT

Life is predictable in that operates under the law of cause and effect. But every now and then, life offers a delightful and encouraging deviation to this law by inconspicuously concealing within it the law of opposite effect. This law, simply stated, goes something like this: In death there is life; when we lose our life, we'll find it; we gain through loss; we are strengthened in our weakness; we increase after we decrease; and, most encouraging of all, we can be exalted in our humiliation.[6] If at the point of our most distressing hour and depressing moments we determine to follow the path of truth, we can, with God's help, turn any condition around.

> *Until we are willing to be changed—or change what we are willing to see is possible—we will be forever bound by our circumstances.*

Never confuse facts with truth. Sure, certain things may have actually happened, but they don't define reality; it's our interpretation of circumstances that defines our reality. Victor Frankl expressed this fundamental principle in his book *Man's Search for Meaning* when he stated, "The last of the human freedoms—to choose one's attitude in any given circumstance, to choose one's own way." He goes on to explain: "Between stimulus and response, there is a space. In that space is our power to choose our response. In our response lies our growth and our freedom."[7]

The only change we can guarantee comes from our own power to choose. Most limitations occur when we establish those limitations as the only viable option we have. Until we are willing to be changed, or change what we are willing to see is possible, we will be forever bound by our circumstances. We must choose to see ourselves, and what we are capable of, differently. Leo Tolstoy so famously said, "Everybody thinks of changing humanity, and nobody thinks of changing himself."[8] Or as the old adage goes: "If we keep doing what we've always done, we'll keep getting what we've always had." If you don't like the circumstances you are currently living in, change them.

Take ownership. Embrace change. Crying over spilled milk doesn't change anything because it is neither creative nor transformative. Explaining every detail of why something happened is a waste of your time and energy. Choosing to clean it up and to find new strategies for avoiding future spills is a more valuable use of your time.

What are your challenges? Identify them and sit with them long enough for God to reveal a solution. And then spring into action! Use what God downloads into your spirit to propel you into a better future.

The more the diamond is cut the brighter it sparkles;
and in what seems hard dealing,
there God has no end in view but to perfect His people.
—THOMAS GUTHRIE

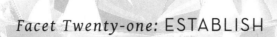

SET YOUR ATTITUDE FOR GREATER ALTITUDE

Best keep yourself clean and bright;
you are the window through which you see the world.
—GEORGE BERNARD SHAW

Life is a journey filled with defining moments, moments that shape our lives and alter the trajectory of our future. On your journey, the greatest gift you can give yourself along the way is the gift of a new beginning. That new beginning starts with renewing your mind—as Paul told the Romans, *"be transformed by the renewing of your mind."*[1] Keep guard over your heart—your attitude—stay hopeful, stay positive, and tap into the power of abundant thinking and a prosperous mindset.[2]

Prosperity begins in the mind and is impossible to cultivate with a negative mental attitude. Your feet will never take you where your mind has never been. You must think peaceful, abundant, and prosperous thoughts before you will experience peace, abundance, and prosperity in your life. You must think successful thoughts if you hope to achieve success. Your success hinges on your perception of your capabilities and potential. Don't allow your thoughts and beliefs to be dictated by your moods, emotions, and feelings. You must persevere in your mind. Perseverance is simply a matter of attitude—of mental fortitude, grit, and single-mindedness. More than anything else, your ability to persist under pressure will land you in the history books and in the halls of fame. In the words attributed to Calvin Coolidge:

> Nothing in the world can take the place of persistence. Talent will not; nothing in the world is more common than unsuccessful men with talent. Genius will not; unrewarded genius is a proverb. Education will not; the world is full of educated derelicts. Persistence and determination alone are omnipotent.[3]

Success is a spiritual and mental process. People who become prosperous believe they will be prosperous. They have faith in their ability to progress and to surmount obstacles. Prosperous people reject self-doubt, fear of the future, and excuse making. They do not pray for success while at the same time thinking thoughts of poverty, practicing a lack mentality, or talking like a beggar and dressing like a pauper. They turn their face toward the thing they wish to accomplish or acquire with unrelenting determination. These types of people also commit to developing the habits necessary for obtaining exactly what they set out to get, accomplish, and become. With relentless determination, they ban any other picture show than the desired outcome from the screen of their minds.

Perseverance is simply a matter of attitude—of mental fortitude, grit, and single-mindedness.

This is exactly what Abraham did when God asked him to sacrifice Isaac, through whom God had promised to *"establish My covenant...for an everlasting covenant, and with his descendants after him."*[4] Now how was God going to establish an everlasting covenant with the descendants of a boy who died before he was able to bear children? He couldn't. So Abraham reasoned *"that God was able to raise him up, even from the dead."*[5] Abraham didn't limp between two opinions, thinking, "How can this be right? God wants me to kill my son? No! Maybe I shouldn't do it..." Abraham instead thought something along the lines of, "Now here is an opportunity to see a miracle! God has promised Isaac's descendants will be blessed—I wonder how He's going to do it? Will He raise Isaac up out of the ashes right in front of my eyes? This is going to be amazing!"

The man who expects prosperity is constantly creating money in his mind, building his mental financial structure to match his financial goals. There must be a mental picture of a desired outcome, a vision that can be clearly articulated. Habakkuk 2:2-3 tells us:

> *Write the vision and make it plain on tablets, that he may run who reads it. For the vision is yet for an appointed time; but at the end it will speak, and it will not lie. Though it tarries, wait for it, because it will surely come.*

If we are going to make it real, we have to wonder about it, we have to meditate on it, we have to write about it, and we have to grab God's promise regarding it. And because God promised it, we must be confident it is forthcoming. In other words, to be prosperous you must maintain a prosperous outlook, you must think opulently, you must feel affluent in thought, and you must exhale confidence and assurance in your very being and manner. Speaking about

> *There must be a mental picture of a desired outcome— a vision that can be clearly articulated.*

your life in prosperous, successful, lavish terms is key. Your mental attitude toward the thing you are striving for and the intellectual effort you put forth to realize it will dramatically impact your chances of apprehending it.

The person who would succeed must think success. You must elevate your thoughts! Colossians 3:1-2 puts it this way: *"If then you were raised with Christ, seek those things which are above, where Christ is, sitting at the right hand of God. Set your mind on things above, not on things on the earth."* You must think progressively, creatively, constructively, inventively, and, above all, optimistically. You must plan your work and work your plan, just as Jesus prescribed in Luke 14:28: *"For which of you, intending to build a tower, does not sit down first and count the cost?"* Have the frame of mind that frames your work. The mental attitude you hold toward your work or your aim has everything to do with what you accomplish.

Your attitude toward any situation or circumstance determines the highs and lows of your life. Your attitude not only increases or decreases your emotional bank account, but also the emotional assets of those around you. The state of your attitude determines the state of your life, your home, your workplace, and your prospects. Your attitude colors your world. Groomed with a positive manner, no person or obstacle can stand in the way of your success or fail to be impacted for the better because they encountered you. William James is credited with saying, "The greatest discovery of any generation is that a human being can alter his life [and the world around him] by altering his attitude."

I once heard a story about an elderly carpenter who was preparing to retire. He told his employer of his plans to leave the house building business and live a more leisurely life with his wife and family. He would miss the paycheck, but he needed to settle down. The contractor was sorry to see this good worker go and asked if he would build just one more house as a personal favor to him. The carpenter said he would, but it didn't take long to see that the carpenter's heart was not in his work. Thinking it no longer mattered how hard or well he worked, he put things together in a shoddy manner and used the cheapest, often most inferior materials he could find to maximize his profit. When the carpenter was finished, the house looked fine, though he knew the poor craftsmanship was sure to cause the new owner a lifetime of headaches.

When the builder came to inspect the house, he patted the carpenter on the back, handed him the front-door key, and said, "You've worked hard for me all these years, so you deserve a reward. This is your house. It is my gift to you."

What a terrible surprise! If he had only worked as diligently as he had his entire career, he would have had a different attitude and produced a different house. Instead, he would now live in a home he would spend his retirement fixing up instead of relaxing in. If you think you don't have time to do something right, think about how much more time it will take if you do it wrong.

We too often build our lives in a complacent and unexpectant way, reacting rather than acting, willing to tolerate less than the best rather than going the extra mile. At important turning points and defining moments, we do not always put forth our best; instead, we hold back. Then, with a shock, we look at the situation we have created and find that we are now living in the house—the ultimate life—we

> *The mental attitude you hold toward your work or your aim has everything to do with what you accomplish.*

have built ourselves. We have raised children we never invested in and have a spouse we hardly know because we have never cultivated those relationships. Many of us will look back with regret. If we had only realized that every action we took, or neglected to take, would affect our future so significantly, we would have conducted ourselves quite differently.

Think of yourself as that carpenter and your life as that house. Every day you hammer a nail, place a board, or erect a wall with your attitude. Build wisely. It is the only life you will be given this side of Heaven, and it may determine the mansion you inherent on the other side.

Play Your One String

Earl Nightingale said, "It is our attitude toward our world...that will determine the world's attitude...toward us."[6] I fully agree. I also think Charles Swindoll said it well:

> Words can never adequately convey the incredible impact of our attitude toward life. The longer I live the more convinced I become that life is 10 percent what happens to us and 90 percent how we respond to it.[7]

> Attitude, to me, is more important than facts. It is more important than the past, than education, than money, than circumstances, than failure, than successes, than what other people think or say or do. It is more important than appearance, giftedness or skill. It will make or break a company...a church...a home. The remarkable thing is we have a choice every day regarding the attitude we will embrace for that day. We cannot change our past...we cannot change the fact that people will act in a certain way. We cannot change the inevitable. The only thing we can do is play on the one string we have, and that is our attitude. I am convinced that life is ten percent what happens to me, and ninety percent of how I react to it. And so it is with you...we are in charge of our attitudes.

Reverend Swindoll also said:

> I believe the single most significant decision I can make on a day-to-day basis is my choice of attitude. It is more important than my past, my education, my bankroll, my successes or failures, fame or pain, what other people think of me or say about me; my circumstances, or my position. Attitude is that "single string" that keeps me going or cripples my progress. It alone fuels my fire or assaults my hope. When my attitude is right, there's

no barrier too high, no valley too deep, no dream too extreme, no challenge too great for me.[8]

Many positive minds become negative by influences that destroy their self-confidence. They gradually lose faith in themselves. However, persistent positive thoughts will increase your faith and positively affect your life—and speaking positively will have a positive impact on your thoughts. I personally have learned the power of making daily declarations and confessions of faith about what I am hoping to achieve. (You can too! Just read through Appendix A out loud for thirty days and see what a difference it makes!)

James 3:3-5 tells us that words are like the bit in the mouth of a horse or a rudder on a ship— they direct our lives. Effective living, success, prosperity, and happiness are a result of mak-

Effective living, success, prosperity, and happiness are a result of making intentional and consistent affirmations regarding the things you want to acquire, accomplish, or achieve.

ing intentional and consistent affirmations regarding the things you want to acquire, accomplish, or achieve. Your words will affect your entire life, destiny, and future—they will mold and shape who you are, what you become, and where you end up in life. Learn the art of positive confession and of visualizing where you want to go, and then actively follow that path. This will dramatically change the way you think and positively impact your attitude.

If you want to think for a change, learn to speak for a change, because your thoughts follow your words and actions as much as your words and actions follow your thoughts. Learn to speak and act "as if" to harness the power of your attitude in persevering through the hardest of times.

The more you tell yourself who you want to be,
the more desire you'll have to be that person.
The more desire you have then,
the more you will tell yourself who you are
[therefore] the bridge between who you are now
and who you want to be
is your words and your desire.[9]
—THABISO WEBSTER TSENASE

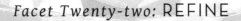

Facet Twenty-two: REFINE

PRACTICE MAKES PERMANENT

If you are going to achieve excellence in big things,
you develop the habit in little matters.
Excellence is not an exception;
it is a prevailing attitude.[1]
—COLIN POWELL

You are a habitual creature. Where you are today is largely a result of your habits. Even your attitude is a habit. Your words and thoughts are a consequence of habit. It's estimated that out of every 11,000 signals you receive from your senses, your brain only consciously processes about forty—and you tend to respond to that limited range based on habit. So, unless you act deliberately, intentionally, and consciously, you'll have the tendency to do the same things today that you did yesterday, the day before, and every day for the last week, month, and year before that.

Habits, good or bad, make you who you are. They allow you to do some things on autopilot so that your mind can focus on more pressing issues. The key is deliberately creating, managing, and controlling those habits so you become the person you want to be rather than one you do not. If you know how to change your habits, then even small adjustments made on a daily basis can significantly alter where you end up in the years ahead.

The Bible tells us that people are constantly tripped up by what they don't know.[2] The new thing you learn today and apply until it becomes a habit may be the very thing that changes everything for your future. By definition, learning is a process of discovering the new—it's getting access to things you didn't know or didn't see in the correct light before. Skills are things you have learned in the past that you turn into habits. They can only be developed over time and acquired through repetition. Just as athletes will do things hundreds of times in a row to develop muscle memory, so we need to practice and repeat the habits we desire so we become more efficient in the little things that make success possible.

Any skill worth mastering requires time and practice. If people can learn the skills of financial underachievement, for example, then it must also be possible for them to learn the skills of being wealthy. In fact, financial management teacher Dave Ramsey explains that people are living hand to mouth because they are doing things that people living hand to mouth do. But if they would start doing what wealthy people do, they would soon find themselves wealthy. It is not just about making more money—it is about what you do with the money you already have.[3]

> *The new thing you learn today and apply until it becomes a habit may be the very thing that changes everything for your future.*

If you don't like the life you have right now, then you need to change your habits. If you're not sure of what to change, find someone who is living how you would like to live and see if you can learn what they do differently. Ask them about their reading or exercise habits, if they can suggest books or classes or new routines; ask if they would be willing to mentor you. Then practice what you learn, allowing time for new skills to develop into habits.

Experts say you need to do something for at least twenty-one days before it changes your behavior, even though some habits may take longer than that. The most significant behavioral change will happen within ninety days. In my experience I have found it takes thirty days to learn a new discipline, sixty days to develop a habit, and ninety days to create a lifestyle.

Research is finding that we can more quickly adapt to new ideas and habit patterns than we previously thought possible. Each new thought and activity physiologically changes your brain by building new dendrites and creating new neural pathways, which means you can, quite literally, rewire your mind in order to think and act like the person you desire to be.

"IF IT IS TO BE, IT'S UP TO ME"

To successfully persevere and press through the hardest of times, you must take ownership for your actions, thoughts, and feelings. Could things be the way they are because you are the way you are? What one or two things can you change that could change everything? Let's start with a change of mind and a change of heart about what is possible. Remember, success is not determined by a condition but a decision. You have to decide to make the change before a change can be made, and then turn that change into a habit.

> *Research is finding we can more quickly adapt to new ideas and habit patterns than we previously thought possible.*

There is no question that by changing your habits you can change the course of your life. Habits are valuable tools. If you had to consciously make a decision about every little thing you did each day, it would be like having to start from scratch from the moment you wake up. Habits help you manage mundane tasks so you are free to learn new things and pay attention to the kinds of decisions that will really make a difference. So understanding how habits work is essential. For that reason, I was eager to read *The Power of Habit* by Charles Duhigg. Here are four tips I believe will help you harness your habits for lasting success:

1. Every habit consists of three elements—cue, routine, and reward.

Together, these three elements form a habit loop. Cue is the thing that triggers you to do the habit, routine is the activity part of the habit, and reward is what you want to obtain by doing the routine. Habit loops work like this: when the *cue* is there, you do the *routine* in order to get the *reward*.[4]

2. To break a bad habit, insert a new routine.

You can't really eliminate a bad habit; you can only *replace* it with a good habit. To do that, you need to insert a new routine in response to the old cue.[5]

Once you identify the cue and the reward of the old habit, you can identify a new routine that can give you a similar reward. You might need to experiment for a while before finding the right one for you. Then you need to make a specific plan about what you will consciously do when the cue presents itself. It might seem simple, but it can be tricky because, by definition, the habit cycle isn't something you are doing consciously. However, studies show that making a plan and persistently applying it does make a difference.

3. To develop a good habit, make a "craving" out of specific cues and rewards.

Let's say you want to develop an exercise habit. Choose a specific cue (like putting your running shoes in a place where you will see them at the same time each day) and a specific reward (such as logging your results). Those won't be enough on their own, but it is where you can start. You also need to make a craving out of them, because cravings are what drive the habit loop. You do that by choosing a reward that appeals to you and allowing yourself to anticipate it. Think about that reward and how good it will be when you get it. Over time it will become a craving and the new habit will become, well, a habit.[6]

4. Keystone habits have a ripple effect.

There are some good habits that can start a chain reaction in all the other habits of our lives. Once you master one such habit, it will affect other areas of your life. Duhigg calls these "keystone habits."[7] Among them, studies show that the habit of exercising your willpower is the most important one. The ability to delay gratification for something better in the future, for example, will have a positive impact on your life overall. This is what Daniel Goleman famously dubbed, "emotional intelligence."

THE BEST TIME TO START IS NOW

Begin right now. There is no better time to start improving your habits than the present. You can start the process by making positive confessions of faith on a daily basis, making daily affirmations about what you are going to accomplish. (Again, see Appendix A for a list of daily declarations to get you started.) Hear yourself speak them out. This exercise will help you build the confidence and commitment you need to persevere. Your words will keep you on the path to the destiny God has waiting for you. So start today!

*Don't be afraid to give your best to
what seemingly are small jobs.
Every time you conquer one it makes
you that much stronger.
If you do the little jobs well,
the big ones will tend to take care of themselves.*
—DALE CARNEGIE

MOVE BEYOND
SELF-DEFEAT

*Perseverance is the hard work you do after you
get tired of doing the hard work you already did.*
—NEWT GINGRICH

For more than a century, psychologists have performed thousands of experiments as they studied human behavior. In
the course of their research, they have come to understand how
deeply rooted psychological patterns and response mechanisms
can be rehabilitated—that certain laws of behavioral change can
have a universal and practical application to the many self-defeating lifestyles of human beings.

Some fifty years ago, knowledge of this behavioral science was
first applied with the introduction of "behavior therapy," a radical
new technique based on the premise that what you do influences
how you think—and feel—about who you are. By changing, or
treating, what appears to be the symptoms of a neurosis—an outward manifestation of an irrational self-defeating behavior—a
therapist can literally change, or *cure*, the thoughts and feelings of
that individual.

Until the emergence of behavior therapy, *behavior* possessed little importance in therapeutic treatment—all therapy was largely rooted in the work of Dr. Sigmund Freud. His psychoanalytical methodology was based on the theory that people are basically helpless until they understand the conflicts residing in their subconscious and the childhood traumas that generated them. As a result, psychoanalytically-oriented therapists assert that it is who you are in your subconscious that determines what you experience and choose to do in your conscious. In other words, your conscious behavior is merely a reflection of your subconscious identity.

Behavior therapy reverses this traditional stance. Simply put, while the psychoanalyst is most interested in pursuing the question, "Why are you this way?" the behavioral therapist is most concerned with, "How can you change now?" Behavior therapy is an action-oriented approach centered on the here and now. All of this is important in the context of our discussion because it specifically addresses the self-defeating mindsets, thought patterns, and emotions that translate into the maladaptive behaviors that may be sabotaging your success.

> *Behavior therapy is an action-oriented approach centered on the here and now.*

If you want to do the hard work of persevering in hard times, then here is what you must do. You must:

1. Embrace the problem as it is in the present moment. Don't lament over it, justify it, or shift the blame for it; simply embrace it.

2. Identify the specific behavior that must be adjusted to resolve the problem. What is that one thing you have the power to change that would result in the outcome you desire?

3. Systematically change the behavior. Focus on what you *can* do, not what you *can't*. Magnify or enhance the future solution over the present difficulty.

The key is to be proactive—to be forward not backward thinking, to be decisive and willing to take immediate action. Behavioral therapy relies mainly, but not exclusively, on methods derived from the psychology of learning and conditioning, and focuses its analysis on observable behaviors rather than on unconscious processes, drives, or conflicts. If a desired change does not take place, the behavioral therapist reevaluates and revises their approach until the desired results are achieved.

> *As you behave and think differently, you will begin to feel differently—you will gain a more positive perception of what is possible based on your inherent worth.*

Cognitive-behavioral therapy holds that a person can exchange bad habits for good ones by deliberately changing their thoughts and beliefs about what is possible. The subject must choose thoughts that are aligned with a desired behavior—while the resulting behavior simultaneously reinforces a corresponding change in how the subject thinks and feels. Modern psychology lends truth to what Socrates advised so long ago: "Endeavor to be what you desire to appear." Acting "as if" outwardly will align your inward thoughts and feelings to that reality.

When you change your behavior, you will change how you think and feel. As you behave and think differently, you will begin to feel differently—you will gain a more positive perception of what is possible based on your inherent worth. At the same time, that very change can cause feelings of anxiety or uncertainty. This of course happens with all of us as we move out of the old and into the new.

Muster the courage to look at your life honestly. Freedom comes when you act by virtue of choice, rather than by mere habit. Regardless of how unsettling those choices may initially feel, you will find that the more you act on them, the more natural they will become. Your greatest obstacle will not be implementing change, but vanquishing fear of that change.

FEAR, THE FINAL FRONTIER

Fear will be your most restricting factor when it comes to making that final push over the finish line. Failure to confront your fears will only cause them to become more debilitating. Step back and take a candid look at any fears or doubts that are keeping you from making a particular behavioral change. Whether it is a fear of rejection, failure, or even success—or some other unsettling result of your action—identify and confront that fear for what it is: a fear of the unknown. This is why it's so crucial for you to articulate your fears. Once you can identify what you're afraid of, thereby giving it a name, it is no longer unknown. Sometimes all it takes is exposing a certain fear to reveal how unfounded it really is.

Changing the fear of the unknown into the fear of something specific will give you the upper hand. Once you are able to name your fear, you will find it's not nearly so frightening. It is when you are afraid even to look that fear gets the advantage over your life. Like a weed, when it is ignored it will take over the garden. Simply taking the time to consider both the negative and positive consequences of any change can be both liberating and empowering. For example, try asking yourself the following questions:

Master the art of change by emphasizing your ability to act, think, and choose differently.

- What is the worst possible outcome?
- How would such a change improve my life?
- What are the pros and cons of the change?

When you are able to acknowledge that a change is worth risking, take the leap! Focus on your strengths. Master the art of change by emphasizing your ability to act, think, and choose differently. Change is simply a matter of choosing to focus on your strengths rather than your weaknesses. When you focus on your strengths, not only will others change their perspective of you, but your perspective of what is possible will change too; you will see new options, opportunities, and prospects that you didn't see before.

Focusing on your weaknesses will prevent you from moving forward. Be gentle with yourself. Be kind and patient. Stop abusing yourself. Stop all self-criticism, because criticism never changes anything. When you criticize yourself, you steep your interior world in negativity, and that negativity will influence everything you experience in life.[1] When you approve of yourself, you will experience change that is positive.

Focusing on your strengths may seem like an exercise in self-deception, but the fact is that a person becomes who they believe themselves to be. Your emotional state emanates from habit-forming thoughts and activities.

THE KEY TO TRANSFORMATION

You are the key to your success. It is not your circumstances or other people—not your position or status—but you. You must take action by exchanging your bad habits for good ones. As we've already explained, to change a bad habit that you have become accustomed to is indeed very difficult. Like a champion who conditions themselves for peak performance—working long and hard for small, incremental improvements—you must condition your mind and strengthen your power of will through strict self-discipline, which will enable you to push through your own inner opposition and the self-defeating limitations that keep you from competing with yourself and winning.[2] You are your only competition.

Self-discipline will move you beyond self-defeat. You can *choose* to do the hard thing, even if you don't *feel* you can. Take the bull by the horns despite your fears and doubts. This can sometimes be exacting, requiring heightened mindfulness, vulnerability, and risk, but the results will quickly reinforce your efforts. Don't overcomplicate the process; self-mastery is simply a matter of harnessing the power of repetition and discipline—and, as behavior therapy tells us, mastering what you repeatedly do will cause you to master how you ultimately feel.

An 1889 article appearing in the journal *Education* published the following statement that summarizes the feeling-behavior-habit loop:

> Feeling issues in action, actions become habit, and habits crystallize into character. The formation of a good character, therefore, is largely dependent upon the right unfolding of feeling.[3]

Your actions, in other words, determine your feelings as much as your feelings determine your actions—these evolve together in a symbiotic dance. Aristotle has been attributed with stating that you become what you repeatedly do, to which we could add that what you repeatedly do determines how you

Mastering what you repeatedly do will cause you to master how you ultimately feel.

feel—or what you believe—about who you can become.

What you acquire and achieve in life is the outward manifestation of who you *perceive* yourself to be and what you *believe* you are capable of achieving. It is never simply a matter of what you want, but of who are. Proverbs 23:7 says, as a man *"thinks in his heart, so is he."*

Although we have learned to tame and domesticate the wildest of animals and master the most treacherous seas and formidable environments, our greatest challenge still remains: how to master our own selves. We can steer elephants and economies, cruise-liners and countries, but what about our daily lives and our destinies?

If you will adjust your attitude accordingly, maintain your strength of purpose, and persevere without wavering, you will be empowered to experience success beyond your wildest imagination.

Out of feelings, it has been said, spring actions;
actions become habit; and habits crystallize into
character. The great functions of the mind should work
in harmony, and should be educated to work so.[4]
—RICHARD G. BOONE

Only those who will risk going too far can
possibly find out how far one can go.[5]
—T. S. ELIOT

Facet Twenty-four: COMPLETE

FINISH WELL

Some people drift through their entire life.
They do it one day at a time, one week at a time,
one month at a time.
It happens so gradually they are unaware of how
their lives are slipping away until it's too late.
—MARY KAY ASH

I have always been inspired by the Olympic motto: *Citius, Altius, Fortius,* which is Latin for "Swifter, Higher, Stronger." The best athletes in the world gather to compete for the gold medal in their chosen event every four years. However, we make a mistake if we think the Olympics are all about competition. Rather, they are about showing an individual's personal best on the biggest stage in the world.

The motto is not "Swiftest, Highest, Strongest"—because the expectation is that every competition will exceed the last, not just as a whole, but for each individual Olympian. For each participant, it is not so much about showing up and doing well as it is about maximizing their personal potential—making that one more push to beat their previous best as they have been doing day in and day out for the four years since the last games took place. It is about incremental improvements adding up to a new personal best and new Olympic and world records.

Many people have great potential, gifts, and opportunities, but they give up or burn out before they finish their race—or worse... they don't even show up.

When I think of the Olympics, it is hard not to think of Usain Bolt. In 2008, he ran his personal best in the 100 meters, finishing in 9.69 seconds to distinguish himself as the fastest man ever to run that race. What was truly incredible about Usain was that two years prior to the Olympics he could not break the 9.75-second barrier, so he pushed harder and longer in his training. All the work he was doing didn't seem to be paying any dividends. He got his breakthrough only after his trainer insisted on rest periods during his rigorous training schedule. He had been pushing his body too hard and doing more damage than good, undermining his own objective. Worried that the rest period would negatively impact his personal routine and the time spent training, he only reluctantly cooperated.

> *As you push forward toward your success, build in times to rest and refuel.*

However, the rest and recovery period actually helped him to perform better on the track and shaved 0.06 seconds off his previous personal best. This may not seem like much, but in a sport like the 100-meter dash, that is the difference between first and second place—and sometimes between Olympic gold and no medal at all.

Just as athletes cannot give their best performance if they train to the point of burnout, you cannot give your best without sufficient rest balanced with consistent training. As you push forward toward your success, build in times to rest and refuel. Resist the temptation to fill the hole in your soul with late night TV or surfing the Internet.

Getting sufficient sleep at night is vital to our rest and refueling. Many of our bad habits—overeating, addictions, etc.—happen in the time after we should already be in bed. Like my mother says, "An idle mind is the devil's workshop." Balance progress with rest, and you will be less likely to succumb to such temptations—you will have both the mental energy and the physical health to push forward with the same Olympic motto of "Swifter, Higher, Stronger" as it applies to your personal goals, aspirations, and objectives.

NEVER GIVE UP

Among plants, Chinese bamboo is unique. When this bamboo seed is planted, watered, and nurtured for a whole growing season, there is nothing that appears above ground. In fact, it takes five consecutive years of cultivation before even the slightest sign of growth occurs. In this entire "dormant" season, not even one sprout will appear. But then in the fifth year, something amazing happens. Within a six-week period, each bamboo plant will grow sixty to ninety feet! All the hard work seems to pay off in the fifth year because it is only then that we see growth, and what amazing growth it is! Now that is an astonishing demonstration of the power of God in nature and the power of the seed in action.

You might ask: "Did the small seed lay inactive for four years and then just come alive in the fifth?" No, the truth is that during the first four years, the bamboo plant was developing underground, expanding its root system. This extensive root system spreads and strengthens during this time, providing an incredible foundation for the tree to shoot skyward in the fifth year. Had the tree failed to build this underground

> *It is in the consistent actions of faith that the "bamboo miracle" works unseen toward realization.*

network of support for four seasons, it would be impossible for it to reach its fullest potential when it was time to push its way heavenward through the soil into the outside world.

This story is telling when it comes to the value of perseverance and of the virtue of unwavering faith. These disciplines are important in the development of the character required to build our own networks of support. We may go through some tough times and see no growth at all, but we have to keep nurturing our character, developing disciplined habits, and building strong relationships. Like growing bamboo, doing these things takes consistency, discipline, faith, patience, and perseverance even in the face of no apparent change. As Henry Wadsworth Longfellow wrote:

> *The heights by great men reached and kept*
> *Were not attained by sudden flight,*
> *But they, while their companions slept,*
> *Were toiling upward in the night.*[1]

King Solomon said something akin to this in the book of Ecclesiastes:

> *As you do not know what is the way of the wind, Or how the bones grow in the womb of her who is with child, So you do not know the works of God who makes everything. In the morning sow your seed, And in the evening do not withhold your hand; For you do not know which will prosper, Either this or that, Or whether both alike will be good.*[2]

There are miracles taking place around us every day, but we don't see how they come about. You may not immediately see the effects of your prayer, of your giving, of the power of a kind word, or of the many other small things that you engage in on a daily basis. You may work to establish new habits and live a moral life and not see the results of those efforts for years. But then, all of a sudden, in one day, the "bamboo plant" you have been nurturing for so long will shoot upward. When did the miracle happen? For the casual observer, they may think it was all of a sudden. But for you, you know the many hours, days, months, and years that you

Live today as if you are where you want to be twenty years down the road already.

labored, sometimes with nothing more than the faith that you were not laboring in vain. The miracle was happening the entire time. Had you given up midway, or even just a few days before the bamboo broke the surface of the dirt, it would have all been for naught.

The book of Hebrews tells us that *"faith is the substance of things hoped for, the evidence of things not seen."*[3] As Christians, we are to live our lives by such faith because it is in the consistent actions of faith that the "bamboo miracle" works unseen toward realization. Just as the bamboo plant breaks through suddenly, I declare that your breakthrough is on the way. What you do today matters— how you grow, what new habits you form, and what problems you confront will have an accumulative effect on your overall success. Like Thomas Edison did when experimenting to invent the light bulb, you may struggle and fail—using a trial and error approach to doing life, fulfilling your purpose, and pursuing your dreams. At times it may seem meaningless and futile, but all of that will change the day the lights come on.

Determine not to miss that moment because you gave up too early. Refuse to be beaten by what life throws at you. Live today as if you are where you want to be twenty years down the road already. Dream it, then wake up and dare to be it. Dare to put feet to your dreams. As H. Jackson Brown put it:

> Twenty years from now you will be more disappointed by the things that you didn't do than by the ones you did do. So throw off the bowlines. Sail away from the safe harbor. Catch the trade winds in your sails. Explore. Dream. Discover.[4]

God has great plans for you (if you don't believe that, then look at Jeremiah 29:11-14). There are miracles, inventions, innovations, new relationships, networks, opportunities, success, prosperity, and breakthroughs awaiting you. Let nothing you face dissuade you from that truth. Use every challenge as a catalyst and stepping-stone to the life of your dreams. Dare. Explore. Dream. Discover.

Look your problems in the eye and say, "Now, just how are you going to make me the person God has destined me to be today?"

In the gospel written by Luke, a story is told of a young boy who wanted to go out and discover life. Pride had derailed his destiny and shame had dropped him to the bottom of the proverbial heap—feeding pigs! When he finally stopped to think about it, *"when he came to himself,"*[5] he realized the lowest servant among his father's employees was better off than he was. That's when he decided to go home. What a difference that one decision made—from a swine-slopper to a celebrated son! Find your way back home and enjoy the benefits of peace and a prosperous life as you rest in the bosom of your heavenly Father. There you will find the wisdom, courage, strength, and fortitude to be the brilliant-cut diamond the world is waiting to be revealed as you persevere through hard times.

Godspeed on your journey to becoming all God has destined you to be.

These are not easy times, but it is a time when you can learn a lot about yourself and your ability to persevere. Make a decision to endure and push through the difficult situations that you face, and you will absolutely have breakthrough. And, when you do emerge from the darkness the light will be brighter, the victory sweeter and the joy more exuberant. It will be worth all the effort, says the Lord. Stay the course.[6]
—MARSHA BURNS

In this you greatly rejoice, though now for a little while, if need be, you have been grieved by various trials, that the genuineness of your faith, being much more precious than gold that perishes, though it is tested by fire, may be found to praise, honor, and glory at the revelation of Jesus Christ.
—1 PETER 1:6-7

Epilogue

DAILY DECLARATIONS AND CONFESSIONS OF FAITH

Compelling scientific evidence proves that our outer realities are mirrors of our inner thoughts. Words are thoughts clothed in language. Words have power, presence, and prophetic implication with no geographical, time, or space limitations. I hereby present you with a thirty-day challenge. Declare these words twice daily—once in the morning upon rising and once at night before retiring—and watch how your brilliance unfolds as every facet of your life begins to reveal God's best concerning you.

Begin by praising God, for you enter His presence with thanksgiving. Thank Him for His promises and His Word at work in you and through you. Consecrate this time by engaging your heart, mind, spirit, and soul. With boldness and conviction speak out the eternal truths found in His Word by declaring the following in faith:

1. I will set my priorities and focus on the things that really matter.[1]

2. I will face my greatest challenges, discouraging situations, and seemingly insurmountable problems with this resolution: "Only good can come out of this."[2]

3. I will practice a positive mental attitude.[3]

4. I will seek the wisdom of God before I make any decision.[4]

5. I will live a life of gratitude.[5]

6. I will honor my word.[6]

7. I will elevate my expectations.[7]

8. I will communicate with honesty and act with integrity.[8]

9. I will diligently love and care for my family.[9]

10. I will practice healthy, positive, successful, and prosperous thinking.[10]

11. I will live authentically.[11]

12. I will be diligent in earning and managing my finances.[12]

13. I will pursue and invest in solid, mutually-beneficial relationships.[13]

14. I will make the most of my time and every opportunity.[14]

15. I will replace unhealthy habits with healthy ones.[15]

16. I will deepen and live out my faith in God.[16]

17. I will maintain a prayerful attitude.[17]

18. I will plan for and model generosity and give to those who can never reciprocate.[18]

19. I will be true to my convictions and core values.[19]

20. I will pursue improvement, refinement, and upgrades in all areas of my life.[20]

21. I will live morally and conduct all of my affairs ethically.[21]

22. I will ensure all of my actions and responses are governed by the Word of God.[22]

23. I will discover and manifest my purpose.[23]

24. I will maximize my potential.[24]

25. I will live life as a visionary thought leader.[25]

26. I will live a holy lifestyle that fosters peace, success, and prosperity.[26]

27. I will give my body the exercise, rest, and nutrition it needs.[27]

28. I will nurture my soul.[28]

29. I will feed my spirit.[29]

30. I will hone my skills.[30]

31. I will walk in forgiveness toward others and myself.[31]

32. I will not grow weary in doing good as I trust God to sustain me.[32]

33. I will give myself permission to prevail.[33]

Every day, in every way, I am growing wiser, stronger, better, and more prosperous.

Living one day at a time;
Enjoying one moment at a time;
Accepting hardships as the pathway to peace;
Taking, as He did, this sinful world as it is,
not as I would have it;
Trusting that He will make all things right,
if I surrender to His will;
That I may be reasonably happy in this life,
and supremely happy with Him
forever in the next.
Amen.
—Reinhold Niebuhr, *The Serenity Prayer*

This is the beginning of a new day. God, You have given me this day to use as I will. I refuse to waste it on maintaining the status quo—I will use it for good. I know what I do today is important, because I am exchanging my time for it. When tomorrow comes, this day will be gone forever, leaving in its place something that I have traded for it. I want it to be gain, not loss; good, not evil; success, not failure—in order that I shall not regret the price I paid for it.[34]

...So, teach me, Lord, to number my days that I may apply my heart to wisdom. Amen.[35]

May the Lord our God be with us as He was with our ancestors; may He never leave us or abandon us. May He give us the desire to do His will in everything and to obey all the commands, decrees, and regulations that He gave our ancestors. And may these words that I have prayed in the presence of the Lord be before Him constantly, day and night, so that the Lord our God may give justice to me and to His people Israel, according to each day's needs. Then people all over the earth will know that the Lord alone is God and there is no other.[36]

ANYWAY

People are often unreasonable, illogical, and self-centered.
Forgive them anyway.

If you are kind, people may accuse you
of selfish, ulterior motives.
Be kind anyway.

If you are successful, you will win some
false friends and some true enemies.
Succeed anyway.

If you are honest and frank,
people may cheat you.
Be honest and frank anyway.

What you spend years building,
someone could destroy overnight.
Build anyway.

If you find serenity and happiness,
people may be jealous.
Be happy anyway.

The good you do today, people will
often forget tomorrow.
Do good anyway.

Give the world the best you have,
and it may never be enough.
Give the world the best you have anyway.

In the final analysis, it is between
you and your God,
not between you and other people.[37]

The virtue of that first command,
I know still does, and will prevail;
that while the earth itself shall stand,
the spring and summer shall not fail.
—JOHN NEWTON

NOTES

PROLOGUE

1. Edward Erlich and W. Dan. Hausel, *Diamond Deposits: Origin, Exploration, and History of Discovery* (Littleton, CO: Society for Mining, Metallurgy, and Exploration, 2002), 74–94.

2. See 2 Corinthians 12:9.

3. Kevin Mullens, *Decisions Decide Destiny* (Hickory, NC: FZM Publishing, 2014), 99.

4. See Proverbs 25:2.

5. See Romans 8:37.

6. See 1 John 4:4.

7. See Jeremiah 32:27.

8. "Brilliant (diamond Cut)," Wikipedia, accessed October 22, 2014, http://en.wikipedia.org/wiki/Brilliant_%28diamond_cut%29.

9. Ibid.

10. Psalm 8:5 states that we have been crowned with glory and splendor. God allows circumstances to chip away at our imperfections so that as the crown of a diamond

reflects light, we are able to unobstructively reflect His glory.

FACET ONE: CLARIFY

1. Please refer to my previous book, *Reclaim Your Soul: Your Journey to Personal Empowerment*. This book will assist you in identifying some of these things.
2. For more insight on the concept of prosperity, please get a copy of my book, *The Prosperous Soul*.
3. For assistance, please get a copy of my book, *The 40 Day Soul Fast*, because it might not be about what you're eating, but what's eating you!
4. See Jeremiah 1:5; Ephesians 2:10; Psalm 139:13-16.

FACET TWO: CORRECT

1. Randy Pausch and Jeffrey Zaslow, *The Last Lecture* (New York, NY: Hyperion Books, 2010).
2. "What Price Glory?" Beliefnet, May 21, 2001, http://www.beliefnet.com/Health/Health-Support/Illness-and-Recovery/What-Price-Glory.aspx?p=1.
3. See John 5:1-10.
4. Conan O'Brien (address, Harvard Commencement, Hanover, New Hampshire, 2011), accessed October 23, 2014, http://www.dartmouth.edu/~commence/news/speeches/2011/obrien-speech.html.

FACET THREE: HEAL

1. Jim Rohn, quoted in Murthy Murali, *The ACE Principle* (Victoria, BC: Friesen Press, 2012), 116.
2. See Samuel R. Chand, *Who's Holding Your Ladder?* (Niles, IL: Mall Pub., 2003).
3. Learn more about Executive Life Coaching™ at www.cindytrimm.com.

4. Go to www.yourlifeeimpowerment.com for a free seven-day trial of the Life Empowerment System.™

5. 2 Corinthians 7:10-11 MSG.

67. See Ephesians 4:15.

FACET FOUR: LEARN

1. Oscar Wilde and Vyvyan Beresford Holland, *Complete Works of Oscar Wilde* (New York, NY: HarperPerennial, 1989), 913.

2. See Luke 8:50; Mark 5:36.

3. See Psalm 23.

4. 1 Corinthians 9:24, 26-27.

5. Epictetus, *Discourses*, Book III, chapter 23.

FACET FIVE: EXPAND

1. Earl Nightingale, *The Strangest Secret in the World* (Seaside, OR: Rough Draft Printing, 2013), 21.

2. James 1:2.

3. Hebrews 12:2.

4. 1 Chronicles 4:10.

5. Vincent Van Gogh, Irving Stone, and Jean Stone, *Dear Theo: The Autobiography of Vincent Van Gogh* (New York, NY: Plume, 1995), 26.

FACET SIX: INSPIRE

1. Connie L. Curran and Therese Fitzpatrick, *Claiming the Corner Office* (Indianapolis, IN: Sigma Theta Tau International, 2013), Introduction.

2. Lee A. Iacocca and Catherine Whitney, *Where Have All the Leaders Gone?* (New York, NY: Scribner, 2007), 11.

3. Seth Godin, *Tribes: We Need You to Lead Us* (New York, NY: Portfolio, 2008), 55.

Part Two: Color

1. Friedrich Wilhelm Nietzsche, Rüdiger Bittner, and Kate Sturge, *Writings from the Late Notebooks* (Cambridge, UK: Cambridge University Press, 2003), 139.

Facet Seven: Adjust

1. James 1:8.
2. Stephen Russell, *Barefoot Doctor's Guide to the Tao: A Spiritual Handbook for Urban Warriors* (New York, NY: Times Books, 1998).
3. See Colossians 1:28; 4:12.
4. See 2 Corinthians 3:17.
5. Howard Thurman, "The Sound of the Genuine" (address, Baccalaureate, Spelman College, April 4, 1980), accessed October 25, 2014, http://www.ptev.org/hints.aspx?iid=4.

Facet Eight: Respond

1. Matthew 13:16 MSG.
2. Romans 8:28,37.
3. Ernest Hemingway, *A Farewell to Arms* (New York, NY: Scribner Paperback Fiction, 1995), 216.
4. James 1:2.
5. Proverbs 3:5.
6. 1 Corinthians 10:13 MSG.
7. Hemingway, *A Farewell to Arms*, 216.
8. Viktor Frankl, *Man's Search for Meaning* (Boston: Beacon Press, 1992), 117.
9. Ibid., 116.
10. Ibid., 85.
11. Hebrews 10:35-36 NIV.

FACET NINE: DEFINE

1. See Isaiah 64:8; Jeremiah 18:4,6; Lamentations 4:2; Romans 9:21.

2. Lydia M. Child, *Letters from New York* (London, UK: Richard Bentley, 1843), 301.

3. See 1 Chronicles 4:10.

4. Napoleon Hill and Arthur R. Pell, *Think and Grow Rich* (New York, NY: Jeremy P. Tarcher/Penguin, 2005), 35.

5. See John 8:32.

6. Gordon W. Allport, *Personality: A Psychological Interpretation* (New York, NY: H. Holt and Co., 1937), 102.

7. Kevin C. Snyder, "The Power of Perspective!" Dr. Kevin C. Snyder, accessed October 26, 2014, http://kevincsnyder.com/the-power-of-perspective.

FACET TEN: CHOOSE

1. Dave Ramsey, *Dave Ramsey's Complete Guide to Money* (Brentwood, TN: Lampo Press, 2012).

2. See Mark 10:27.

3. See Matthew 19:26; Mark 9:23.

4. Denis Waitley, *Seeds of Greatness* (New York, NY: Pocket Books, 1984), 87.

FACET ELEVEN: INVEST

1. See 1 John 4:4; 2 Corinthians 4:7.

2. See Psalm 23.

3. See Hebrews 13:5.

4. See Luke 15:11-24.

5. See Ephesians 3:20.

6. See Ephesians 1:19; 3:7.

7. Galatians 6:8 MSG.

8. See James 4:10.

9. Isaiah 55:6-8.

10. See James 1:5; John 16:13.

11. See Luke 11:13.

12. See 2 Peter 1:10.

FACET TWELVE: ENVISION

1. Frankl, *Man's Search for Meaning,* 116.

2. See Mark 10:27.

3. See Romans 12:2.

4. See Philippians 4:6.

5. Wayne W. Dyer, *The Power of Intention* (Carlsbad, CA: Hay House, 2004), 173.

PART THREE: CARAT

1. Betty Friedan, *The Feminine Mystique* (New York, NY: Norton, 2001), 463.

FACET THIRTEEN: MEASURE

1. See Isaiah 43:4.

2. Douglas Harper, *Online Etymology Dictionary,* s.v. "purpose," accessed October 26, 2014, http://www .etymonline.com/index.php?term=purpose.

3. Mary Wollstonecraft Shelley, Betty T. Bennett, and Charles E. Robinson, *The Mary Shelley Reader* (New York, NY: Oxford University Press, 1990), 16.

FACET FOURTEEN: DIFFERENTIATE

1. See Ecclesiastes 3:1.

2. Leinz Vales, "Watergate figure, Christian leader Chuck Colson dies," CNN US, April 21, 2012, http://www.cnn .com/2012/04/21/us/chuck-colson-obit/index.html.

3. Charles W. Colson, *Born Again* (Old Tappan, NJ: Spire Books, 1977).

4. Theodore Roosevelt, "Citizenship in a Republic" (speech, The University of Paris, Paris, France, April 23, 1910).

FACET FIFTEEN: TRANSCEND

1. William Arthur Ward, "To Risk."

2. Pausch, *The Last Lecture*, 108–109.

3. Letter to Morris Raphael Cohen, March 19, 1940.

4. "Coyotes Introduce Gretzky as Coach," ESPN.com, August 9, 2005, http://sports.espn.go.com/nhl/news/story?id=2128903.

5. Catherine Pratt, "Inspirational Stories," Life with Confidence, accessed October 30, 2014, http://www.life-with-confidence.com/inspirational-stories.html.

6. Ibid.

7. John F. Kennedy (address, University of Maine, October 19, 1963).

8. Jo Coudert, *Advice from a Failure* (Lincoln, NE: IUniverse, 2003).

FACET SIXTEEN: FORTIFY

1. See 2 Timothy 1:7.

2. 1 John 4:4 NLT.

3. Hosea 4:6.

4. George C. Mitchell, *Matthew B. Ridgway: Soldier, Statesman, Scholar, Citizen* (Mechanicsburg, PA: Stackpole Books, 2002), 20–21.

5. Joshua 1:6-8.

6. 1 Peter 1:13.

7. See 1 Corinthians 15:57.

8. See Numbers 13:30.
9. Philippians 1:20 NLT.
10. 2 Chronicles 19:11 MSG.
11. Joshua 1:9.

FACET SEVENTEEN: CAPITALIZE

1. See the poem "Invictus" by William Ernest Henley.
2. John Patrick, *Prelude to Chaos* (Xlibris Corporation, 2009), 12.
3. Kurt Goldstein, *The Organism: A Holistic Approach to Biology Derived from Pathological Data in Man* (New York, NY: Zone Books, 1995), 162.
4. Ibid.
5. Clenard Childress, "We Hold These Truths to Be Self Evident," Renew America, June 25, 2010, http://www.renewamerica.com/columns/childress/100625.
6. Martin Luther King Jr., quoted in Wolfgang Mieder, *"Making a Way out of No Way": Martin Luther King's Sermonic Proverbial Rhetoric* (New York, NY: Peter Lang, 2010), 126.
7. Martin Luther King Jr., "The Three Dimensions of a Complete Life" (speech, New Covenant Baptist Church, Chicago, Illinois, April 9, 1967), http://mlk-kpp01.stanford.edu/index.php/kingpapers/article/the_three_dimensions_of_a_complete_life/.
8. Melissa Rattle, "Bridge the Gap," The Church on the Square, February 12, 2008, http://www.tcots.org/about-us/news/monday%27s-with-melissa_33251.html.
9. 1 John 1:5.
10. Matthew 5:14.
11. Childress, "We Hold These Truths."

12. Karol K. Truman, *Feelings Buried Alive Never Die* (Las Vegas, NV: Olympus Printing, 1995), 9–10.

13. Ibid.

14. See Mark 11:22-24; Romans 14:22-23; Hebrews 11:1-40.

15. See 2 Peter 1:4; 1 Corinthians 2:16.

16. 2 Corinthians 4:7.

17. Matt Ridley, *Genome: The Autobiography of a Species in 23 Chapters* (New York: Harper Collins Publishers, 1999), 7.

18. Hebrews 10:7.

19. 2 Peter 1:4.

20. Jiddu Krishnamurti, *Think on These Things* (New York, NY: Harper & Row, 1964), http://www.jiddu-krishnamurti.net/en/think-on-these-things/1963-00-00-jiddu-krishnamurti-think-on-these-things-chapter-20.

21. Thomas Byrom and Ram Dass, *Dhammapada: The Sayings of the Buddha* (Boston, MA: Shambhala Publ., 1993), 1.

FACET EIGHTEEN: INTEGRATE

1. Heath L. Buckmaster, *The Magical Adventures of Princess Carrina* (Transaltar Publishing, 2011), 7.

2. See 2 Corinthians 3:18.

3. Colossians 1:27.

4. Steve Maraboli, *Life, the Truth, and Being Free* (Port Washington, NY: Better Today, 2009), 36–38.

5. Patrick Rothfuss, *The Name of the Wind: The Kingkiller Chronicle: Day One* (New York, NY: DAW Books, 2007).

6. Philippians 4:8-9 MSG.

7. Mark 4:24; Luke 6:38 MSG.

8. Henry David Thoreau and Joseph Wood Krutch, *Walden, and Other Writings: By Henry David Thoreau* (Toronto, Canada: Bantam Books, 1962), 360.

9. See Romans 8:28.

10. 2 Peter 1:10-11 MSG.

FACET NINETEEN: EXPOSE

1. John Webster, *The Duchess of Malfi* (Mineola, NY: Dover Publications, 1999), 91.
2. See James 1:4.

FACET TWENTY: REVEAL

1. Romans 5:3-4 NIV.
2. Romans 8:28, 37.
3. Margaret J. Wheatley, *Finding Our Way: Leadership for an Uncertain Time* (San Francisco, CA: Berrett-Koehler Publishers, 2005), 262.
4. See 1 Chronicles 4:10; Isaiah 54:2.
5. See Exodus 31:3; Isaiah 11:2-3.
6. See 1 Peter 3:18; Mark 8:35; Philippians 3:7; 2 Corinthians 12:9; Joel 2:25; Matthew 23:12.
7. Frankl, *Man's Search for Meaning,* 75.
8. Leo Tolstoy, *Pamphlets: Translated from the Russian* (Christchurch, UK: Free Age Press, 1900), 29.

FACET TWENTY-ONE: ESTABLISH

1. Romans 12:2.
2. See Proverbs 4:22-27.
3. Elizabeth Knowles, *The Oxford Dictionary of Quotations* (Oxford, UK: Oxford University Press, 1999), 236.
4. Genesis 17:19.
5. Hebrews 11:19.
6. Nightingale, *The Strangest Secret,* 42.
7. Charles R. Swindoll, *Swindoll's Ultimate Book of Illustrations & Quotes* (Nashville, TN: Thomas Nelson, 1998), 38.

8. Charles R. Swindoll, *Man to Man: Chuck Swindoll Selects His Most Significant Writings for Men* (Grand Rapids, MI: Zondervan Pub. House, 1996), 64.

9. Thabiso W. Tsenase, "The Power of Positive Words," Motivateus.com, February 10, 2012, http://www .motivateus.com/stories/power-of-positive-thoughts.htm.

FACET TWENTY-TWO: REFINE

1. Oren Harari, *The Powell Principles: 24 Lessons from Colin Powell, a Legendary Leader* (New York, NY: McGraw-Hill, 2003), 14.

2. See Hosea 4:6.

3. For more on this, I urge you to check out Dave Ramsey's Financial Peace University courses. You can learn about these at http://www.daveramsey.com/fpu.

4. Charles Duhigg, *The Power of Habit: Why We Do What We Do in Life and Business* (New York, NY: Random House, 2012), 20.

5. Ibid.

6. Ibid., 36.

7. Ibid., 100.

FACET TWENTY-THREE: ENHANCE

1. See Proverbs 4:23; 23:7.

2. See my book by the same name: *PUSH: Persevere Until Success Happens Through Prayer.*

3. Thomas J. Morgan, "Training the Sensibilities," *Education* 9, no. 5 (January 1889): 298.

4. Richard G. Boone, *Science of Education* (New York, NY: C. Scribner's Sons, 1904), 309–310.

5. T.S. Eliot, "Preface" to Harry Crosby, *Transit of Venus: Poems* (Paris, France: Black Sun Press, 1929), ix.

Facet Twenty-four: Complete

1. Henry Wadsworth Longfellow, "The Ladder of St. Augustine," *Birds of Passage*, 1847.

2. Ecclesiastes 11:5-6.

3. Hebrews 11:1.

4. H. Jackson Brown, *P.S., I Love You* (Nashville, TN: Rutledge Hill Press, 1990), 13.

5. Luke 15:17.

6. Marsha Burns, "Small Straws in a Soft Wind," *Spirit of Prophecy* (blog), September 19, 2014, http://www.hiskingdomprophecy.com/spirit-of-prophecy-bulletin-september-2014/

Epilogue: Daily Declarations and Confessions of Faith

1. See Matthew 6:33

2. See Romans 8:28

3. See Romans 12:2; 1 Corinthians 2:16

4. See Proverbs 3:5-6

5. See Ephesians 5:20

6. See James 5:12

7. See Ephesians 3:20

8. See Ephesians 4:25

9. See 1 Timothy 5:8

10. See Philippians 4:8; Joshua 1:8-9

11. See 1 Chronicles 29:14-19; Matthew 5:43-47; John 1:19-23; 4:23-24 MSG

12. See Proverbs 6:6; 13:22

13. See Ephesians 5:1-2, 21; Romans 12:10

14. See Ephesians 5:15-16

15. See Romans 12:1-2

16. See Hebrews 11:1; Mark 11:24

17. See Ephesians 6:18

18. See 2 Corinthians 8; Deuteronomy 15:10

19. See Matthew 16:26

20. See Philippians 3:12

21. See 2 Peter 1:5, 17

22. See Deuteronomy 12:28

23. See Romans 8:28; 2 Timothy 1:9

24. See Hebrews 3:1

25. See Proverbs 29:18; Jeremiah 23

26. See Hebrews 12:14

27. See 1 Corinthians 6:19-20; Hebrews 4:11

28. See Jeremiah 50:19

29. See Acts 20:28

30. See Exodus 31:5

31. See Colossians 3:13

32. See Galatians 6:9; 2 Thessalonians 3:13

33. See Joshua 1:8

34. Author Unknown.

35. Psalm 90:12.

36. 1 Kings 8:57-60 NLT.

37. Reportedly inscribed on the wall of Mother Teresa's children's home in Calcutta, and attributed to her. However, an article in the *New York Times* has since reported (March 8, 2002) that the original version of this poem was written by Kent M. Keith (see http://www .paradoxicalcommandments.com/origin.html).

DR. CINDY TRIMM'S
EMPOWERMENT
SERIES

UNCOVER YOUR ASSIGNMENT AND PURPOSE,
HIDDEN IN YOUR SPIRIT.

WWW.CINDYTRIMM.COM

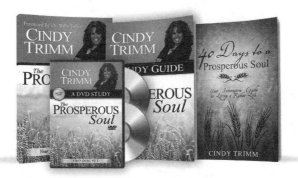

CindyTrimm.com
Let's stay connected!

CINDY TRIMM

Be sure to visit us online at *CindyTrimm.com* for lots of online resources to empower, equip and encourage you daily!

Videos • Blogs • Articles

Speaking Event Schedule • TV Broadcast Information

Online Resources • Email Subscribe

...and more!

 @cindytrimm

 facebook.com/drtimm